Unmasking Deception

A Modern Guide to Media Literacy in an Age of Misinformation

Written and Published by Aaron Jaeger

Aaron Jaeger

Copyright © 2024 All rights reserved.

No part of this publication may be copied, reproduced in any format by any means, electronic or otherwise, without prior consent from the copyright owner and publisher of this book.

Table of Contents

The Urgency of Exposing Media Manipulation in a World Divided by Misinformation 4

Part 1: The Psychology of Media Manipulation 7

From Subtle Bias to Outright Lies 22

The Right-Wing Pipeline 37

Doublespeak in Action 49

Bridging the Divide: The Perception of Elitism 56

Part 2: The Tools of the Trade 70

Traditional Media's Long Shadow 71

Social Media's New Reality 75

Visual Lies 83

Working for the Machine: Everyday Complicity 95

Part 3: Becoming Media Literate 103

Breaking the Echo Chamber 115

Building Truth-Based Communities 120

Part 4: Taking Action 125

The Art of Honest Dialogue 129

The Educated Rebel 138

Part 5: The Role of AI – Promise and Peril 142

The Perils of AI in Misinformation 143

The Promise of AI in Truth-Seeking 150

Conclusion: Rebuilding Trust, One Truth at a Time 156

The Urgency of Exposing Media Manipulation in a World Divided by Misinformation

Let's start this book off on a positive note - the world is a mess. And unfortunately for us the people who are supposed to help us understand what's going on - the media - are often the ones making the mess worse.

You don't even need to stretch yourself too far to see how the media manipulates our understanding of truth. Every day, we're bombarded by outlandish headlines, outrage provoking images, stories, articles and content crafted to make us feel something, anything really, other than at one with ourselves in a calm sane state. And that's just in traditional "mainstream media" let alone on social media, where algorithms have turned everything into clickbait for the masses, feeding off our biases for the sake of engagement.

But rest assured; we're not completely helpless in this. In fact, this is exactly why I'm writing this book. Because the more we understand about how the media works and how it manipulates us, the more power we have to stop it. And we need to stop it - not just for the sake of facts and truth, but for our ability to think clearly, act reasonably, make sense of the world we're living in and come together as a united community.

I'm sure we're all well aware that media manipulation isn't some abstract, theoretical problem. It's real, it's been happening since the dawn of time and it's happening more effectively right now than it ever has before. We all see the media machines feeding us conspiracy after conspiracy, machines and algorithms that only bow to their one true god - ad revenue. And the people in charge of the media don't give a damn about the truth. They care about power, profits, and pushing their own agendas.

But here's where it really sucks, while the oligarchs sit on high pulling the strings. It's the everyday person who doesn't even know they're being manipulated that really pays the price, and the rest of us that have to live with the outcomes of these lies. You may even believe you're one of the smart ones, who can see through the bullshit, but it's more than likely that you've brought your fair share of snake oil in your time too. So, if you're reading this, chances are you're someone who wants to break free from the cycle of misinformation, but maybe you're just not sure where to start.

This book is here to show you how to recognise the lies, spot the patterns, and start taking action. The truth is, we're all caught in this web of deception. It doesn't matter if you're on the left, right, or somewhere in the middle. The media doesn't actually care about your political beliefs, your values, or even the truth. It only cares about keeping you engaged - getting you pissed off, scared, or confused enough to keep clicking, watching, and consuming.

But it's time to fight back. Not with anger or frustration, but by arming yourself with understanding and knowledge. This is about learning the tricks, the psychological shortcuts, the biases that the media is using to manipulate you - and then saying "No, thanks."

This book is divided into five parts, each aimed to take you deeper into understanding the media manipulation around you and how to fight back.

In Part 1, we're going to break down the psychological tactics the media uses to get inside your head. You'll learn how they play with your emotions, twist the facts, and craft narratives that leave you questioning what's real.

For Part 2, we'll dive into the tools of the trade - how the media operates behind the scenes, from the power of social media algorithms to the role of corporations and political groups in shaping the narrative.

Part 3 is all about spotting the patterns, giving you the power to separate fact from fiction. This is where you'll learn to critically evaluate what you see and hear in the media.

In Part 4, we're going to talk about taking action. This is where the rubber meets the road, how to have honest conversations, hold the media accountable, and make sure you're part of the solution, not just a passive victim of the problem.

Then finally in Part 5, we'll get into the boogeyman discussion of AI, and how that is shaping the narrative today and into the future.

So, throughout this book, we're going to dive deep into the mechanics of media manipulation. We're going to break it down, step by step, so you can start to see the patterns and recognise the manipulation for what it is. But we're also going to talk about how to break free. How to think critically, question what you see, and take action in a world that's flooded with lies.

But fair warning because once you start seeing through the lies, you'll be able to make better choices, have better conversations, and maybe, just maybe, help others see the truth too.

Are you ready? Because it's time to stop being manipulated.

Part 1: The Psychology of Media Manipulation

"The most effective way to destroy people is to deny and obliterate their own understanding of their history."
— George Orwell

As much as Cersei Lannister might claim that "power is power," in today's world, the most powerful weapon is not really physical force - its control over information, or as Littlefinger argued "knowledge is power." Because when you have control over information you seldom need to resort to physical force to enact your agendas, if you do then it's either come as a result of, or as a last resort to, the information that has been shared. And in the hands of those who seek power, the media has become the most effective tool for shaping our reality.

The media doesn't simply report the news, it never really has. It creates the news to suit agendas. It takes facts and spins them into stories. It takes emotions and amplifies them into outrage. It takes truths and distorts them into propaganda. And it does all of this with one primary goal; to control how we think and what we believe.

You might like to think that you're an independent thinker, that you form your own opinions based on the facts. But the reality is, our minds are being manipulated in ways we can't always see. Media companies know exactly how to play on our emotions, our biases, and our deep-seated fears. And they're not doing it for your benefit. They're doing it to keep you hooked, keep you angry, and keep you coming back for more. Because in a world driven by clicks, views, and ad revenue, your engagement is the product they're selling.

So let's get started in pulling back the curtain and explore the psychological tricks the media uses to manipulate us. You'll get a clear picture of how they exploit our biases, trigger our emotional responses, and play on our deepest insecurities. My hope is that by understanding these tactics, you can start to recognise when you're being played - and, well, stop falling for it.

The Psychology of Persuasion

When you flick on the evening news, scroll through your social media feed, or maybe you're in the slim minority who still pick up a physical copy of the daily newspaper, what's really happening? Sure, you're consuming information, you might be even entertained, but importantly you're also being sold something. And I'm not even talking yet about the ads for some new miracle weight loss supplement, some crappy pillow or the latest celebrity perfume. I'm talking about your time, your attention, and ultimately, your beliefs.

The media uses tactics that are soaked in psychology at every level of what they do and you have to remember that they're not here to just keep you updated and informed, their whole task is to persuade you. Once you understand these tactics they use, you'll see them everywhere. So, let's break down the psychological tricks the media pulls to sell you on believing what they want you to believe.

Scarcity and Fear: "Hurry, This Is About to Disappear!"

Starting out with the absolute classic, one that is deep-seated in human evolution, we have scarcity and fear - which is stunningly effective. When something is limited - whether it's time, resources, or even information - our brains naturally perceive it as more valuable. The classic example here is diamonds, which are not actually as rare as what we've been led to believe. The powers that be who control the diamond trade, hold back the release of all the stock to create the impression that they are indeed "rare gems" and for generations we've been fooled into believing this, therefore like the suckers we are, we splash out ridiculous amounts of cash on an item that holds considerably less value.

The use of scarcity when it comes to news media is the same as in advertising, which triggers a sense of urgency and a 'fear of missing out' aka FOMO. Suddenly, we're not just passive consumers of information; we're desperate to know it before it's too late.

Take a look at how news outlets operate. They'll often frame a situation in a way that makes it seem like an opportunity or piece of information is fleeting, or that something crucial is about to change. Think about the constant headlines about "breaking news." The goal? To get you to stop scrolling and pay attention right now, before it's "gone." It's not just about urgency - it's about creating a feeling that you need to act fast or risk being left out.

This tactic is especially potent in politics. How often do we see stories framed as "make-or-break" moments - where a single vote, bill, or decision will determine the course of history? In these cases, it's not about informing you; it's about getting you emotionally hooked so you can be manipulated into acting on that urgency.

In sales and marketing this tactic alone can account for a huge percentage of sales for any business throughout the year. Think back to the last time you saw an ad that said the product was discounted for a "limited time only" or the "sale ends soon"? Suddenly, you felt that little spark of panic, right? You didn't want to be the person who misses out, so you bought it, even though you may not have needed it. Congratulations, you just fell for the scarcity principle.

You may have even recognised that they were using this tactic, and even though that little voice in your head was telling you it's ridiculous, you still did some mental gymnastics to justify the purchase. "Well, I will save 25 cents if I buy it now, so I'd be silly not to, right?"

And this isn't just some sleazy tactic used by dodgy infomercials at 3 a.m. or by seemingly every online course under the sun. No, it's a core principle of advertising, and when it comes to drumming up a sense of scarcity and fear, politicians are the GOAT. Think about the messaging you hear around election time - candidates often scapegoat minorities as coming to take your jobs, their political rivals as coming to take away your freedoms. They try to frame the argument like somehow there's only so much liberty and freedom available, so you have to vote for them to protect the little that you have. They'll discourage their opponents' economic plans by creating the sense that spending that might benefit another will take away spending that might benefit you. The goal? To create a sense of urgency, scarcity and fear in order to get you to take action without thinking it through too much.

Take Black Friday, for example. Companies slap a "limited-time offer" tag on something, and suddenly people are willing to trample each other in a mad rush to get a deal on a TV they don't need. Well, politicians do the same thing - bombarding you with "urgent" election updates, making you feel like if you don't vote, everything will collapse. Scarcity is a tool, and it works near every damn time.

One of the reasons scarcity works so well is the FOMO we mentioned, keyword fear. Fear is a close ally to scarcity, and can be used separately or as a deadly duo, but let's look at fear itself.

Fear, from an evolutionary standpoint has been hugely beneficial, you would most likely have heard the term "fight or flight" before. This basic instinctual reaction kept us humans from being devoured by a sabre toothed tiger. Very handy indeed. However, since it is such an engrained reaction, fear has also been used to sell us on ideas time and again throughout history, and those that want to manipulate you know this trigger point all too well.

Like all emotions though, fear is an emotion that can come and go, if you're aware of it you can actually visualise it leaving the space of your mind. Fear is unique though as it's an emotion that can, more easily than others, draw you deep within and keep you in that state. It can send you spiralling into other negative emotions of anger, anxiety, jealousy and hate.

So when you're being sold on a message of fear, you need to train yourself to react rationally. Take a breath, take a moment or two to absorb the information, remove yourself from the coal face and think deeply about why that emotion was triggered and what motive those selling you the message might have for them to poke that pain point?

Especially when it comes to political and social matters, negative emotions such as fear, anger and hatred can best be nullified by empathy, reasoning and understanding. Putting yourself in the shoes of others, and trying to find a compassionate answer to the problem you're being presented.

Often scarcity and fear are used to drum up a sense of competition, you must have this item before others get it, you must not let others take that next step on the ladder or your position is at stake.

Really we need to stop comparing each other as though we're climbing ladders, or up a stairway to some mystical end point with finite resources. Instead imagine we're all on an even pathway, each moving towards their own goal, some may be a few steps or miles in front or behind you, but we're all simply on the journey at our own speed. No reason to fear or be in competition with one another, when we can all simply celebrate and cheer on each other's accomplishments.

Authority: "Trust Me, I'm an Expert"

Another tactic the media uses is leveraging authority. It's simple, when someone with perceived authority tells us something, we're far more likely to believe it. Whether that's a doctor, a scientist, a politician, or a talking head on the news, we're conditioned to trust experts - especially when they sound confident and are backed by credentials.

This is a method that I myself have used, and I've encouraged clients of mine to use it as a substantial reason for jumping on social media. The theory goes that the more you're seen talking about your given subject, the more likes, comments and followers you can accumulate, the more likely it is that others will see you as an authority on the subject. Therefore they'll buy your course, or product, or whatever it is you're selling. And it works extremely well. I'm not going to use any names here to keep myself out of the courts but I'm sure you can think of famous television "doctors" who have created a career and amassed great fortunes by, firstly starting out as the "experts" brought in on world-famous talk shows, then graduating up to starring in their own television shows. Well, you might be shocked to know that some of these "doctors," and yes I'm using the word doctor in quotation marks, have had their medical practice licences revoked, or they never held a doctorate within the field of expertise they claimed in the first place.

So I'm sure you can see the catch here - authority doesn't always mean truth. Media outlets use this to their advantage by presenting individuals who appear knowledgeable or experienced, even if their expertise is questionable. Much like the TV "doctors", think about the pundits who are wheeled out on news shows to waffle on about politics, as though they have all the answers.

At the end of the day it's not about being right. It's about appearing right. And because humans are wired to trust figures of authority, we often fall in line without questioning whether the authority figure is actually trustworthy.

Traditional media has used this for generations, and social media jumped right on this trend from the moment it was formed and it's now grown to such an extent that it's invasive to our culture as a whole. It's like a snake eating its own tail now, where someone builds a following on social media so much so that traditional media knows they'll get eyeballs on their channels if they interact with that creator, so those social media gurus are suddenly presented as the expert on mainstream news media.

It's insanity, to the highest order.

The truth is, we all trust people who are presented as experts - whether they're wearing a lab coat, presented on the news or hell, anyone with a podcast microphone these days.

In advertising, this is why brands love to drag out celebrities to sell their products. When there's a Kardashian with perfect skin, holding up a bottle of face cream, telling you that it's the secret to their flawless complexion? What they're really saying is, "Trust me - I'm a credible authority on beauty." But in reality; Just because someone's a celebrity doesn't mean they know jack about skincare or politics for that matter. What they do know is how to read a script believably.

And when it comes to political campaigns? Authority is the ultimate power move. Politicians use the "expert" angle all the time. They bring in economists to talk about fiscal policy, military generals to talk about national security, or scientists to talk about climate change. They make sure you know they've got the "best and brightest" backing them up, even if their so-called experts are only experts in getting paid to push a particular agenda or just their own circus of celebrity endorsements.

Social Proof: "Everyone Thinks This Way, So It Must Be True"

Ever noticed how many people seem to adopt the same opinions, beliefs, or even product preferences as everyone around them? Odd right, that you'd somehow manage to grow up Christian in a western nation, and Islamic in a Middle Eastern one right? That's the power of social proof, the sophisticated big brother of peer pressure. If everyone else is doing it, it must be the right thing to do, right?

Did you ever have a parent say to you, "If all your friends were jumping off a bridge, would you jump too?" and you thought, well yeah must be fun if everyone's doing it? That's social proof in a nutshell right there, and somewhat the innocence of youth.

The media uses social proof constantly. They'll show you polls, surveys, and focus groups that suggest "everyone agrees" with a particular point of view. Even when that poll shows that barely 51% responded in favour, they'll still wrap that in language like "the majority agrees." Scrapping over halfway is hardly what should be considered a majority but they're betting that you'll forget the actual figure and take to heart the argument is simply that the majority agrees.

They'll display the number of followers, likes, or retweets a particular opinion has received. The more people who support it, the more it seems credible. It's the classic "mob mentality" at work. When you see a hashtag trending, or a viral post that gets thousands of likes, there's a subconscious pressure to jump on the bandwagon and if you don't like something that everyone else does, either you'll feel like the outcast yourself or people will treat you as though you are.

Some people will go so far as to wear the alternative opinion as a badge of honour, using it as though it's a personality trait to be edgy - which is a whole other psychological issue going on.

But social proof is a double-edged sword. Just because a large group believes something doesn't make it true. It simply means people are more likely to conform to the majority opinion. The media knows this, and they exploit it by creating the illusion that everyone is on board with their narrative, whether or not it's actually the truth.

Think about it. If the whole world started to tell you that drinking your own pee was actually really good for your health, at first you might be rightfully disgusted. If you kept noticing that everyone felt this way, you'd start questioning your sanity. Eventually you might be worn down by the sheer amount of people telling you this is true and encouraging you to try it. If you grew up never being told any different, you probably wouldn't even question it. If you've currently got your nose turned up in disgust even thinking about that idea, I'm sorry to tell you but there are currently people who believe this and consume this, shall we say - beverage?

This social proof method is usually pretty easy to spot - and you see it every day on social media. The moment something goes viral, it's like the floodgates open and suddenly, everyone and their dog is talking about it. Whether it's the latest dance challenge on TikTok, a hashtag trending on Twitter, or a viral video that's gotten millions of views - social proof is everywhere.

In advertising, it's the ultimate sales tactic. Consider for a moment what you think about product reviews. If you saw 5000 five-star ratings on a product, you'd be more likely to buy it, right? Why? Because you assume that if so many people are buying it, and rating it so highly, it must be good.

Movie studios have used this for decades, where they'll proudly display the awards that the movie has won or the star ratings of reviewers, even if they're paid for reviews. And today they use it in a really odd way that's as see through as cellophane wrap. Where they'll flash a bunch of "five-star" reviews on screen so that your eye only has enough time to catch how much it must be loved by reviewers, only to find out, if you pause, that the review is from some random nobody on Twitter. But they often get away with this because the general movie goer just sees a flood of five star ratings and that seals the deal, they're off to watch the latest Dwayne Johnson flick.

Politicians use social proof in a way that's even more dangerous. Ever seen a political ad that shows "average" voters raving about how much they love a particular candidate? Or maybe they flash poll results with 90% approval ratings. That again is social proof at work - making you think that everyone else is on board, so you should be too. This creates a sense of belonging. If everyone else is supporting this candidate, then maybe you should, too. It's powerful stuff, especially when it plays on vulnerable desires to be part of the group.

And in politics, the more vulnerable the group, the more susceptible they are to this group think. It can start small with literal paid actors to stand in and fill the frame of a campaign video and appear to be actual supporters, you garner the support of a dedicated minority and start to instil certain language, certain actions and even certain style of clothing. You consistently hit them with a barrage of the same messaging and talking points, simple yet effective slogans. In time, when you have stadiums filled with people goose-stepping to your ideals, those who may be on the fringe, being that solo voice in a crowd of thousands. It's easy to learn to goose-step then it is to argue back.

These psychological tricks are the backbone of modern marketing and media manipulation which has led us to this "group think" that we see now more than ever, the "us vs them" style of politics that has permeated every aspect of our social lives. It's designed to keep us scared and trust only what is fed to us within our own little bubbles and social circles.

You're Not Just a Consumer - You're a Target

Now, none of this is to say that all media is inherently evil or malicious. But it is to say that the media, as it exists today, is constantly working to manipulate you. Whether it's using scarcity and fear to make you feel that urgent sense of dread, authority to make you fall into line with the current hot topics, or social proof to make you feel like you're in the wrong if you disagree, the end goal is always the same - to control your attention and, ultimately, your thoughts.

Remember, whether it's a pair of shoes you don't need or a politician's promises that sound too good to be true, you're always being sold something. And if you think you're immune to this kind of manipulation, think again. We all fall for these tactics - even the best of us. So don't worry, there's no shame if you're sitting there right now thinking back on the many instances you yourself have been suckered in by these tactics.

These messages can end up sitting deep within the recesses of your mind and even if you are aware of them, habit can still dictate that you fall for it anyway. Sometimes you may even allow yourself to take the bait because the thing being sold seems minuscule in the scheme of things. You saw an ad last week for Baskin and Robbins, and ever since have craved a scoop of cookies and cream in a waffle cone, so the moment you pass the store, why not give yourself a treat? Harmless, unless of course you're fighting to lose weight.

Other times those messages can be more invasive and detrimental to not only your own self awareness and mental health but to society in large. If you've ever caught yourself demonising another group within our society for all or at least some of our collective woes then you may want to pause and take stock of the situation and ask yourself if you're coming from a place of empathy and total awareness, or are you parroting talking points like a South Park character yelling "They took our jobs!"

The key to defending yourself and overcoming these tactics is awareness. The more you understand how scarcity, fear, authority, and social proof are used to manipulate you, the easier it is to step back and ask yourself, "Do I actually want this, or am I just reacting to psychological manipulation?"

Once you start to recognise these tactics, you'll be much harder to manipulate. You'll see past the smoke and mirrors, and instead of being an easy target, you'll become a savvy consumer of information.

In the end, the media, advertisers, and political campaigns are all playing the same game. They're trying to influence you in ways that are often subtle and hard to detect. But when you learn how to spot these tactics, you can stop being a passive pawn in their game - once you've got that down, it's game over for them and game on for you.

Checklist for Spotting Manipulative Tactics

Now that you're armed with the knowledge of how scarcity, fear, authority, and social proof are used to manipulate you, let's break it down into an actionable checklist. This will help you spot these tactics in real-time wherever you may face them in the real world or online.

1. Is there a sense of urgency? Scarcity is all about making you feel like you have to act now or miss out. Ask yourself, is the message trying to create a feeling of urgency or panic? Does it seem like you'll regret it if you don't act quickly?

    If it feels rushed, there's a good chance you're being manipulated into making an emotional decision.

2. Is this about your emotions or logic? Manipulative tactics love to play on your emotions because they're easier to trigger than your logic. Ask yourself, if I remove fear, excitement or anger from this equation, what would my rational mind think? And if I looked at this issue with empathy, how would I respond?

If a subject brings up strong negative emotions, take a step back, calm yourself and try to think rationally about why that is, and what motive the message has in bringing those emotions to surface.

3. Who's the expert? Who's speaking, and why should I trust them? And are they just wearing the title, or do they have actual knowledge to back it up?

   If the "expert" doesn't seem to have relevant credentials or if their arguments are vague, you're probably being sold an image of authority, not actual truth.

4. What's the group think at play? Does the message imply that "everyone" agrees with this, and if you don't, you're an outsider? Or is the content making you feel like you're missing out or being left behind if you don't join in?

   If the message is pushing you to conform to a "group opinion" without giving you room to think for yourself, it's social proof in action.

5. Does this feel like a sales pitch? Whether it's a product, a political candidate, or an idea, if it feels like you're being sold something, then you probably are. Ask yourself, are they selling you a lifestyle, identity, or image, instead of reality?

   If it feels like they're more interested in making you feel something than giving you the full picture, you're being marketed to.

Not Everything is a Conspiracy, But Verify First

The key to not being manipulated is a healthy dose of awareness and scepticism. The next time you're presented with information - whether it's a news story, a political ad, or a product recommendation - run it through this checklist. If it triggers any of those red flags, slow down. Ask questions. Dig deeper. Take a minute to breathe before you act. It's easy to get swept up in the rush of emotions, the persuasive power of an expert, or the fear of missing out. But when you know how these tricks work, you can step back and make decisions that are based on rational information, rather than pure emotion.

Remember, you're not a passive consumer of information. You're an active participant in the media landscape. Once you start spotting these manipulative tactics, you'll see them everywhere. And the best part? You'll stop falling for them.

From Subtle Bias to Outright Lies

When it comes to media manipulation, often it's not about flat-out lying. The more obvious a lie, the easier it is to be caught out and if you're caught out, like for example Fox News was with the Dominion voting machine stories they ran with, you open yourself up to lawsuits. Which in the case of the voting machine lawsuit ended in a settlement with Fox owing over $700 million dollars. So, it's best not to tell outright lies, in favour of massaging the truth.

The real masters of deception are those who know how to frame a narrative - twisting the language, imagery, and even numbers to make the truth seem like whatever they want it to be.

We're talking about the fine art of persuasion, where it's not so much about the facts - they know they can't hide those - but about how those facts are presented. Because let's be honest, you can make the same set of facts look like two completely different stories depending on how you tell it.

As the great philosopher of our time, Homer Simpson would put it, "Facts are meaningless. You could use facts to prove anything that's even remotely true".

Language: The Power of Framing

Words hold a lot of power, and can be wielded like a weapon, especially when using them to evoke an emotional response. The way news outlets can use language to frame a story can be quite subtle and sneaky. You can make something sound incredibly tragic or just another day at the office by tweaking a few key words.

As an example, let's look at how a protest or rally story might be covered. Just the difference of referring to the people attending that rally as "protesters" versus "rioters." What images are brought to mind when you hear those words?

Sure, technically both words refer to people involved in demonstrations, but for me "rioters" brings up the image of burning piles of rubbish on the street, stores being looted, clashes with police, hooded and masked vigilantes out causing trouble. While the word "protesters" brings up images of hippies camping out, peaceful marches in the street, well organised and lawful demonstrations. So what word an outlet chooses really matters and sets the tone for the entire narrative. And they're not stumbling upon the use of these words by accident, they're carefully workshopping and selecting the ideal words to provoke the appropriate reaction.

Remember the media's coverage of the Black Lives Matter protests in 2020? Depending on the outlet, the same events were described in completely different terms. Fox News used phrases like "violent mobs" or "looting and chaos," while CNN and other outlets would refer to them as "peaceful protesters" or "calls for justice." Same event, but with different language used to sway your perception. One made you think of destruction and anarchy, while the other made you think of peaceful civil disobedience.

This isn't a coincidence. The media knows that words carry emotional weight and can prime you to view a situation through a particular lens. And when we live in a world of non-stop, 24/7 news coverage, the repetition of those words and particular phrases can really soak into your mind, and suddenly you find yourself repeating these catch phrases with all the fundamental understanding of them that a parrot has repeating "polly wants a cracker".

This framing isn't just found in news media, brands know this tactic all too well. I'm sure I could list a few major brands right now and you'd think of their slogans directly from their ad campaigns without fault.

Like when I bring up the brand of McDonalds for instance, what immediately springs to mind? If you're from a certain generation you may have just started singing the Big Mac song in your head. In more recent times though, at least at the time I'm writing this book, you probably thought of "I'm lovin' it". The framing of such a phrase is about as subtle as being smacked over the head with a sledgehammer.

Love? That's a strong emotion, some say it makes the world go around. So this massive brand is using that to directly tap into that part of your brain and hopefully as you're stuffing down their burgers and fries followed up with a thick shake, there's that little part of you thinking "I'm lovin' it," because hey, love will make you do crazy things right? Like, continually go back to junk food for that little fuzzy feeling inside that was planted in your brain well before you brought the burger.

Imagery: Picture the Story You Want to Tell

Next, let's talk about imagery. You've heard the saying, "A picture is worth a thousand words," right? Well, when it comes to media manipulation, those thousand words are often tailored to fit the narrative. The media doesn't just report facts; they select images and footage that reinforce a particular angle.

Consider political campaigns. They're not just visiting the store to pick up some donuts, they want to capture an image or video of the interaction that paints them in a good light. We've all seen the set up of a politician kissing a baby, so much so that it's become almost entirely a cliche at this point. What about those times they head out to visit regional electorates and speak to farmers wearing a long-sleeve shirt but with the sleeves rolled up and top button undone, or they're visiting industrial workers wearing the high vis vest and hardhat, or in Australia the one we see every election cycle is the candidate having a beer at the local pub, that's not an accident. The images are meant to create an emotional connection - a loving family man, a down to earth person just like us or in the case of the pub example here in Australia that's meant to signify a major voting question of "Would I share a beer and yarn with this person?" for if you can't do that, they're deemed untrustworthy, regardless of what's actually being said or done.

Take the image of a politician giving a speech in front of a crowd. Depending on the angle of the shot, the number of people in the frame, and the lighting, you can make it look like they're speaking to thousands or just a handful of dedicated supporters. The difference between an image with a full crowd and one with a half-empty auditorium can significantly impact the public's perception of the politician's popularity.

One that always makes me laugh is when politicians hold press briefs out on the campaign trail, you can probably picture it right? The politician is standing in front of a bus which is wrapped in their party's branding and key election slogan, there's supporters dressed in their colours holding campaign placards behind them, and the politician themselves stands there addressing the media's questions. The reason these make me laugh is because 99% of these press huddles are completely manufactured, and while the shots that are shown in the press are of what looks like a crowd of supporters gathering around their candidate, if you simply move back a few feet it would reveal that there is nothing more to see other than the press themselves. It's all a silly little media farce.

Just this year in 2024, when Donald Trump was running for president, we all saw the assassination attempt and the now famous image that followed, where Trump was standing defiantly in front of the American flag, fist pumping in the air and blood spilled across his face. Now, love or hate the guy, staged conspiracy or not, that photo right there may have won him the presidency and will certainly remain in history books for generations to come.

But for now let's take a step back again from the heated political sphere and into the level headed world of social media. Sarcasm absolutely intended.

As a marketer who has been operating in the industry through the final years of televisions absolute domination of the marketing world and who has not only witnessed but been very much a part of the world of online social media advertising from the outset, the control these social media platforms have and to the degree in which their algorithms operate would truly shock most.

A quick history lesson on television advertising is in order to demonstrate this.

TV networks used to sell advertising "spots" aka the placement of where the ad would be shown during certain programs or events. They'd sell certain spots, for example the Super Bowl, at a premium because they'd claim that x amount of viewers would be watching.

Now, the tricky part here is they didn't really know how many people would be watching, it was all just based on averages. They had these black boxes installed in certain homes throughout cities and towns to try to accurately represent the demographics of that area, from that they'd extrapolate what the viewer numbers of any given program or event was but there was only ever one box per household, so a family that may have had a television in their living room which the parents watched and one in a spare room that the kids would watch wouldn't accurately be able to track what the kids watched.

Much different to the modern era where social media, apps and websites track every click, scroll, and second viewed.

As a marketer back in that old era of television you'd rely on common tropes and themes with ads, want to sell the latest make at home taco pack? Have a happy family sitting around a dining table eating and smiling happily together. Then you could only really gauge how good that campaign was working as the sales figures started to come back, which could take months to properly understand the impact.

But with the power of social media and the tracking abilities they have, the numbers can't lie. You can deep dive into every metric, right down to the most minute detail and you have the ability to split test everything.

Take for example the same taco product. The algorithms tell us, in no uncertain terms, that an ad featuring mixed race families, outside or in well lit environments and all smiling will perform much better than one that features a single person without a smile. Because that's what the social media platforms want their feeds to look like - a bunch of happy smiling people.

So when media outlets, politicians and advertisers can use this knowledge to such a fine degree of detail, you best believe that every image you see is specifically designed, edited or chosen to elicit the exact response that they want from you.

At the end of the day images are just as much a tool for manipulation as words.

Statistics: Lies, Damn Lies, and Data

Finally, we get to the heart of the deception, statistics. There's an old saying: "There are three kinds of lies - lies, damn lies, and statistics." Numbers can be twisted, bent, and manipulated to say whatever you want them to say. Which to most people would come as a big of a surprise, surely 2+2 always equals 4 right?

The problem isn't necessarily the numbers themselves, it's that most people are terrible at interpreting statistics. We don't have the time or energy to break down complex data, so when a news outlet flashes a statistic at us, we tend to just accept it as truth - especially if it aligns with what we already believe.

So the tricky part is that numbers can be presented in a way that misleads or distorts reality. Maybe the number is correct, but the context is completely off. Or maybe it's a cherry-picked statistic designed to reinforce a specific point.

During political debates, you'll often hear candidates or pundits throw out statistics like, "Unemployment is at an all-time low!" or "The crime rate has decreased by 20%!" These numbers might be technically true, but without context, they may be meaningless. For example, a "20% decrease" in crime sounds impressive, but if you were starting from a point where crime was already at historically low levels, a 20% decrease could mean only a small reduction.

They may have chosen to show that 20% reduction zoomed in on a certain time period. But if you zoom out you'd see that the previous 4 year period crime soared to all time record highs, so the 20% reduction now is simply bringing it back into alignment with historical normals.

Context matters. But most media outlets don't give you the full story - they just give you the cherry-picked number that fits the narrative.

Or consider the classic argument of climate change, surely no data has been misused or misrepresented here, right?

One common argument by climate change sceptics, aka those who deny its effects, involves highlighting short-term periods where global temperatures appear to plateau or even slightly decrease, despite the long-term warming trend. The narrative being that "Global warming has stopped."

In the early 2000s, sceptics frequently pointed to the period from 1998 - 2012, a time when global surface temperatures increased more slowly compared to previous decades. They claimed this showed that global warming had "paused" or even ended.

There's some not so subtle manipulation going on here though as 1998 was an exceptionally hot year due to a very strong El Niño event, skewing the starting point for comparisons. By choosing 1998 as the baseline, sceptics created the illusion of a pause in warming, even though the overall long-term trend showed continued temperature rise.

When viewed over longer periods, say 50-100 years, the data clearly shows a steady upward trajectory in global temperatures. The "pause" was merely a statistical artefact caused by cherry-picking a specific timeframe.

Not to be biassed in this cherry picking, on the pro-climate action side, some advocates have at times exaggerated short-term impacts to drive urgency with some activist groups and media headlines around the early 2000s warning of dramatic

sea-level rises, up to several metres within two decades, causing immediate and widespread devastation.
These claims sometimes highlighted worst-case scenarios from high-end projections in reports like those from the IPCC, without accounting for the range of uncertainties or the slower pace at which these changes are likely to occur.

So while the data does in fact point to a scientific consensus, that sea-level rise is indeed happening and poses significant long-term risks, the rate has been closer to 3-4 millimetres per year. Catastrophic multi-meter rises will take centuries under current projections, though this does not diminish the urgency of addressing root causes.

I'm sure you can see how tricky reporting on data can get, and there's probably a number of you reading this now fuming either for or against the narrative of which side lies the most and blah, blah, blah. That's not the point here, the point of both examples is to show how statistical data can be selectively presented to fit a narrative. On one side sceptics have exploited short-term fluctuations to downplay long-term trends. And on the other side activists have amplified worst-case scenarios to evoke emotional responses or drive policy action.

The solution to this statistics problem is media literacy, a healthy level of further enquiry and a focus on scientific consensus, which evaluates data over appropriate timeframes and considers the full range of probabilities. And when considering scientific reporting this really brings us full circle back to language, as it's quite rare for a scientist to ever state an absolute fact with the way they describe truths. People often misunderstand the term 'theory' in a scientific sense, compared to an everyday sense. Science is a practice that by its very mode of non-stop enquiry is in a constant state of flux, so gravity is a theory in so much as the current hypothesis of the theory of gravitation has never been proved wrong. If someone were to be able to prove it wrong, under strict scrutiny from the wider scientific community, then the theory would change.

So, you might notice when scientific experts are asked if something is 100% true, they'll use phrases like "that's the current understanding," or "that's what the data indicates." They're not saying it's wrong, but they're always open to the research being proven false. Which leaves them open to get picked apart from media that has alternative motives, because they'll use that refusal to stand behind 100% certainty as proof the theory is wrong. It's a tricky tactic that you should be on the lookout for.

Remember, the media, advertisers, and politicians don't always outright lie. Instead, they might look at what they're doing as little white lies, a small stretch of the truth. They manipulate the way you see things by framing the narrative in a way that benefits them. They use language, imagery, and statistics not necessarily to inform you, but instead to guide your perception of reality.

So, next time you read a headline, watch a political ad, or scroll through a newsfeed, remember this; The truth isn't just something that's presented to you as-is. It's something that's often framed, shaped, and twisted to fit someone else's agenda. Your job is to recognise when it's happening and dig deeper to get the full picture.

Don't let them paint a picture of reality for you. Grab the brush, and start creating your own.

Guide to Reading Between the Lines

Now that you're aware of how language, imagery, and statistics are used to manipulate you, let's look at some practical tools for reading between the lines. The media loves to present you with a neatly packaged version of reality, but your job is to peel back that packaging and see what's really going on.

Here's your guide to spotting when you're being fed a manipulated story:

1. Look Beyond the Headline.

    Headlines are designed to grab your attention and push your buttons. But here's the problem, they often don't reflect the full story. Headlines are clickbait, pure and simple. They're written to spark emotion and make you want to read more. But the real substance is usually buried deeper in the article or omitted entirely.

    So don't judge a story by its headline. If the headline seems overly sensational or extreme, take a second to think, "What are they really trying to get me to feel here?"

    Then take the time to actually read beyond the first few sentences. Get into the actual content of the piece. See if it contradicts or provides context for the headline.

    Like, if a headline reads, "Crime Rate Soars Under New Policy," ask yourself, Soaring by what measure? Is it a small uptick in a city that's already seen a decrease in crime? Or is it a massive jump in one specific neighbourhood? Don't be fooled by vague generalisations - dig deeper.

2. Check for Loaded Language.

    Remember that language is a weapon. Words have a huge emotional impact, and journalists and advertisers use them to push you in one direction or another. Words like "radical," "extreme," "out of control," or "unprecedented" are usually indicators that the article is trying to manipulate you emotionally rather than presenting facts.

You need to keep a look for emotionally charged words and ask, Why are they using this language? It could be present in the tone. Is the writer trying to get you to feel fear, anger, or hope? If so, that's a sign that you're being pushed to a conclusion without the full context.

As an example, a news piece might say, "The president's policies have resulted in catastrophic economic consequences." But if you dig into the data, the supposed "catastrophe" might only be a temporary dip in a very complex issue. So while the word catastrophic immediately stirs up fear, making you feel like something terrible has happened. Is it actually that bad? Or is it just the way they're telling it?

3. Examine the Source - Who's Behind This?

When reading any article or watching a news segment, ask, Who's behind this? Is it a trusted news source, is it a blog post, or is it purely an opinion piece with a clear political or commercial agenda? Who is benefiting from this information being spread, and why?

With any information presented to you, you have to check the credibility of the source. Is the publication or outlet known for its objectivity? Are they affiliated with a specific political or corporate group that might shape their narrative? Consider the funding or backing. If it's a political ad, for instance, look at who's paying for it. The money behind the message matters.

And at the end of the day, if the information and data is being presented without sourcing its references. Then it's not worth the paper, or digital pixels it's written on. Real information will always lead to real sources, not a rabbit hole of other biassed articles, but peer reviewed data, statistics or published findings in reputable publications.

Take for instance if you're reading a study on healthcare policy, is it funded by a pharmaceutical company with something to gain from the outcome? Or is it a peer-reviewed study conducted by an independent research organisation? Don't take every source at face value. Dig into who's funding or publishing it.

4. Scrutinise the Statistics.

As we talked about, statistics can be manipulated easily. A number might look convincing at first glance, but you need to ask, What's the context? What's missing? Numbers don't speak for themselves; they need context to mean anything.

So check the sample size and method. Look into how this data was collected, was the sample large enough to be reliable? Was there any bias in how the data was gathered? And look for the baseline. How does this stat compare to past data? Is there a change over time, or is it an isolated figure? Is it part of a bigger trend or just a spike in one area?

A report might claim that 80% of people support a certain policy, but what they might not tell you is that the sample size was only 100 people in one small town. So if that was the case, is that statistic representative of the broader population? Most likely, not.

5. Consider the Opposing Viewpoint.

   Finally, always try to get a second opinion. If you only hear one side of the story, you're missing half of the picture. Biassed reporting happens when only one narrative is presented, and you're not given the full scope of what's going on.

   So with the world at your finger tips, seek out alternative sources. Look at the same story from a variety of outlets and perspectives. Then truly try to understand the other side. Even if you don't agree with it, try to understand the reasoning behind the opposing viewpoint. It's how you build a fuller, more accurate picture of reality.

   If you read an article bashing a new government policy, search for opinions from those who support it. What reasons do they give? And are those reasons valid or just parroting the narrative that's been pushed on them? You'll be surprised how much you can learn by looking beyond your viewpoint and trying to consider the full picture in good faith.

To truly see through the manipulation, you've got to slow down and analyse what's being presented to you. Read between the lines, not just the headline. The next time you pick up a piece of news, take a second to ask the questions we've outlined here. Look for subtle manipulations in language, imagery, and stats. Dig deeper into the source of the information. Seek out alternative viewpoints to broaden your perspective.

By doing this, you're not just consuming media - you're actively engaging with it. You'll be able to spot bias, question the narrative, and uncover the hidden truths lurking beneath the surface.

And remember, in a lot of the back and forth that you're presented with on a daily basis online and on televisions, it's generally just the loudest voices that are being heard. The majority of people are a lot closer in values than you may think. So while there are those who may have ill intent in shaping the narrative, trying to paint the world in extremes, most people are just trying to navigate the lies that we're all bombarded with each day, so always try to start from a place of kindness to your fellow man, aim to come towards an understanding and strive for a world of unity and compassion.

The Right-Wing Pipeline

While I would strongly argue that most people sit further towards the centre of the political divide than most may think, I would also have to argue that there's something uniquely insidious about how people get pulled into extremist online echo chambers. It doesn't happen overnight. It's a slow burn - a series of small steps that eventually lead someone down a rabbit hole that's hard to crawl out of. And the biggest driver of this process? Social media algorithms. These things are designed to keep you scrolling, keep you watching, and most importantly, keep you hooked on more extreme content.

It starts innocently enough. You're scrolling through your feed, catching up on the latest viral video or news story. But once the algorithm catches wind of what you engage with, it starts feeding you more. Maybe it's a funny meme or a video that aligns with your views on the economy. But over time, your feed becomes increasingly tailored to one thing, polarising content.

The Algorithmic Trap: How It Works

As we all know, well surely we at least have some clue of the basic level, social media algorithms work by tracking your behaviour - things like what you click, what you watch, and how long you linger on a post. These algorithms have a very simple main goal, to keep you engaged. And the easiest way to do that is by showing you content that reinforces your existing beliefs.

But there's a giant issue with that. The more you engage with content that confirms your biases, the more the algorithm shows you content that pushes you further along the same line. Of course by now you would have heard the term "Echo Chamber", this is where your views are constantly validated, and being validated is a great feeling. Who wants to be made seem a fool or publicly shamed? Now that I write that I'm certain there's a kink out there that fits that description. However, for the most part we want to feel right, we want to feel accepted by our peers. So once you've been drawn in these echo chambers then make it harder and harder to break free from the cycle.

Let's say you're casually browsing YouTube and you watch a video about the economy. Maybe it's a conservative pundit explaining how the government is wasting taxpayer money. You don't think much of it, may have found the discussion somewhat enlightening, but the algorithm notices you watched the whole video. The next time you open YouTube, it shows you another video - this time a more radical take, calling for the end of social welfare programs. You're intrigued, so you click. As you watch, YouTube suggests even more extreme videos - ones that push conspiracy theories or anti-government rhetoric. Over time, your feed is flooded with content that feeds into the idea that the system is broken and that only radical solutions will work.

This is exactly what's happening and it's not just YouTube. Facebook, Instagram, TikTok - all of these platforms use similar algorithms to trap you in a feedback loop. And the more polarising the content, the more likely you are to click, comment, or share it. Because let's face it - controversy sells.

And the silly thing here is that the platforms don't really care about the standard of discourse within that engagement, so if people start arguing on articles, videos or posts that are clearly rage bait, the algorithms don't care. It's just a simple computation that this post has seen x amount of comments and engagement, or this video has x amount of retention in watch time, which equals that post or video being boosted.

So a really simple thing you can do to limit the reach of information you don't like, and to avoid being trapped in an echo chamber is to simply not engage. The less people that comment and engage, the less the algorithm will boost that reach, so the less people that will be potentially sucked into bad information and echo chamber nonsense.

However, once someone is caught in the algorithm's trap, it's easy for people to slowly drift towards more extreme ideologies. The more they engage with this polarised information the more they begin to engage with the communities surrounding it. Those ideologies are then reinforced by those communities of like-minded people and suddenly it's not just the content but it's the social pressure that encourages users to dive deeper.

Social media groups and forums play a huge role in this process. These spaces, often disguised as "free speech" zones, create an environment where extremist ideas are normalised and even celebrated. Whether it's a Facebook group, a Reddit thread, or a Discord server, or even a streaming service, these online communities start to echo each other's ideas, pushing members further toward radical beliefs.

Over time, the user becomes more entrenched in the group's ideology, finding themselves isolated from friends and family who might not share the same views. If you're being shunned by one community, whilst another is welcoming you with open arms, it becomes a natural choice to align yourself with the people that accept you. The algorithms then continue to push people towards even more extreme content, until they're completely immersed in a bubble that has very little connection to reality.

One of the truly dumbest things about all this is that some of the most well known movements in the past decade online have been started as a joke. By literal teenagers, just messing with people. They present things as factual and create a whole ideology around them that preys on people's desire to feel like they're "on the inside", that they have the real information, and that they're special for "seeing the truth." When in reality it was a group of teenagers on Reddit having a laugh and seeing how far they could take it.

The "Us vs. Them" Mentality: The Power of Group Identity

One of the most dangerous aspects of the right-wing pipeline is the tribalism it actively encourages. Once you're in these groups, you stop seeing the "other side" as simply different - you start seeing them as the enemy. Social media amplifies this "us vs. them" mentality, which is perfect for political radicals looking to stoke division.

The more time you spend in these echo chambers, the more you start to see the world in binary terms, you're either with us, or you're against us. And the more extreme the rhetoric, the easier it is to demonise those who disagree with you.

This is why social media influencers or conservative pundits often refer to people who disagree with them as "liberals," "snowflakes," "socialists" or even "vermin." It's a way of dehumanising the "other side," making it easier for followers to rally behind the speaker's ideology without questioning it. When the "other side" is painted as evil, dangerous or less than human, it justifies extreme measures, from online harassment to actual real world violence.

Using this type of dehumanising rhetoric is straight out of the tyrants playbook. I'm sure those that know what I'm talking about are expecting me to reference a certain "Austrian painter" to demonstrate my point but it's much, much older than his movement.

The fall of Rome happened because of who? The Barbarians! What a viscous, filthy hoard they must have been - right? That's certainly what the Romans would have us believe via their telling of history.

In the early middle ages the British Isles were plagued with attacks by bloodthirsty pagan Norsemen and women. Savages the lot of them.

The Greeks and the Persians, the Gauls and the Huns, the Egyptians and the Hittites. Demonising the "other side" as less than human, uncivilised or barbaric is a tale as old as time.

It's something that almost runs in our blood, and from an evolutionary standpoint would have its share of benefits back in hunter gatherer times. Humans have been on this planet for approximately two hundred thousand years, with agriculture sparking the appearance of true civilisations only being approximately twelve thousand years. So for the majority of our existence we've been composed of small tight knit communities and run-ins with other tribes could have been seen as a danger for security of your tribe, a fight for resources that were by no means guaranteed.

So it's theorised that this "us vs them" mentality has been engrained in our way of living for so long, that even in modern times where we have more understanding of the complex structure of our intertwined cultures than ever before, there's still a part of us that is easily triggered by a fear of others. We still separate race by surface level descriptions, separate borders by arbitrary lines and so it's still incredibly easy to stoke division along political and ideological lines.

It's time we move past that caveman thinking towards a brighter future.

Don't Let the Algorithms Control You

Surprise, surprise, but I'm sorry to inform you that social media algorithms don't care about your well-being, they care about engagement. The more time you spend scrolling, the more they profit. And nothing gets more engagement than outrage and division. So, they'll keep showing you content that stirs up anger and reinforces the idea that "your side" is right and "the other side" is the enemy.

If you want to avoid getting sucked into the pipeline, you need to start questioning the content that's being served to you. Look at your feed critically. Are you only seeing content that reinforces your views? Are you only interacting with people who think the same way you do? If so, it's time to step outside your echo chamber.

Diversify your sources. Follow people from different political backgrounds, listen to podcasts from multiple perspectives, and read news from a variety of outlets. And I'm not suggesting you have to take on the far right or left of any topic, there's great resources out there that can help you find more trustworthy sources that sit further towards unbiased, central views on topics. Then when you find those sources, support them. The more we vote with our attention and engagement, the more the conversation will steer towards the centre.

Trust me, I know that listening to some of the opposing viewpoints can feel like pulling teeth, especially when you land on the far side of any group. And even though I'm encouraging diversity in opinion that doesn't mean you have to listen to the extremes where outright hateful and bigoted opinions often fester. I'll admit I have blocked a lot of the creators on those extremes because in the end we still must hold the discussions to a level of civil discourse, and once they move towards calls for outright hatred, or shift into dog whistle type language that signifies real world harms then I can no longer support with my attention.

By blocking such content it does signify to the platforms that those creators should attract less attention. And I would encourage to find voices on both sides of any issue or political divide that hold themselves to a higher standard of debate, to support a move towards that type of dialogue as a whole.

So, how can you finally step outside the algorithm's grasp? Use social media less. Use it more mindfully. Make sure you're actively seeking out diverse content, not just passively scrolling and engaging in rage bait.

The right-wing pipeline is powerful, but it's not unbeatable. You don't have to get swept up in the flood of polarising content. By being more conscious of how the algorithms work, and by seeking out alternative perspectives, you can free yourself from the ideological bubble and regain control over what you consume online.

I'm sure there's those of you reading right now thinking that I myself am being biassed right now, by only focusing on the right wing pipeline - don't worry, the other side is coming.

Case Studies of Prominent Figures and Misinformation Networks

To truly understand how the right-wing pipeline operates, I'd like to take a look at real-world examples - people who have played a key role in spreading misinformation and polarising audiences. These individuals often don't operate in isolation; they're part of a network of influencers, media outlets, and online communities that work together to amplify a particular message.

By dissecting how these figures operate, we can see just how powerful the pipeline really is.

For legal reasons I'm going to choose to not share the names of these figures, as they're a very litigious bunch, but you'll still get an understanding of how they operate and what to look out for. You may think of this as a Jeopardy of right wing pundits and networks, where sadly you may also be able to associate quite a few names to the same stories.

The Master in Misinformation

This particular man is one of the most infamous examples of how an individual can leverage the power of social media and online platforms to build a massive following. As the founder of an online news platform, he became a one-man misinformation factory, spreading conspiracy theories about everything from the 9/11 attacks to the school shootings. His platform was built on the foundation of fear-mongering, scapegoating, and outright lies.

His rise to prominence shows how misinformation can be amplified when you build a narrative that taps into people's deepest fears. He didn't just spread random conspiracy theories; he carefully crafted a worldview in which the mainstream media, government, and global elites were all part of an organised effort to suppress the "truth." The more outrageous his claims, the more they spread. Why? Because they evoked emotional reactions - people either bought into them or felt compelled to push back. Either way, it generated engagement.

Take a certain school shooting hoax, for instance. Sadly school shootings are all too common in America but during the aftermath of one of these events this man claimed it was a "false flag" operation, a staged event used to push a political agenda. Despite the overwhelming evidence to the contrary, his claims spread like wildfire across social media. Followers rallied around him, while others were radicalised into believing that major tragedies were faked. This is what's called narrative amplification in action, a false claim, made with enough conviction, that spreads far beyond the original source, gaining traction as more and more people share it.

He has since been sued into bankruptcy for this claim and his online news platform has been sold off to support the payout to the victims parents and school.

Echo Chamber of Conservative Ideology

The next gentleman is another prominent figure who's built a massive following by leveraging polarising content. Known for his quick-witted arguments and controversial takes on social issues, he has managed to build a vast online presence, particularly among younger conservatives. His rapid-fire delivery and bombastic style have made him a social media sensation, but his appeal lies in reinforcing a particular ideological narrative.

His messaging revolves around the idea of "facts don't care about your feelings", which resonates deeply with people frustrated by what they perceive as the left's political correctness. But what he often does is simplify complex issues into soundbites that reinforce conservative viewpoints, while framing liberal perspectives as intellectually lazy or even dangerous. This, in turn, has polarised audiences, encouraging them to see the world through the lens of us vs. them.

His frequent critiques of social justice movements or progressive policies are often framed as arguments for rationality and against "emotion-driven" politics. By constantly positioning himself as the defender of reason, he draws in followers who want to feel intellectually superior to those on the "left," thereby deepening the ideological divide.

He has made a name for himself by also debating those with opposing views and posting those clips online, often these debates involve himself taking on college kids on campus. His fast talking style and his ability to, what his followers might refer to as "dunk" on these debate opponents presents him as an intellectual heavy weight. However when presented with actual debaters or experts in their fields his arguments are often easily unravelled and exposed for the shallow rhetoric it is.

The Network: Normalising Extremism

This particular "news" network, led by prominent far-right figures, has been instrumental in spreading populist and far-right rhetoric. It was one of the first media outlets to embrace alt-right ideologies, framing them as legitimate alternatives to mainstream political discourse. It's not just about reporting the news; it's about creating a narrative that casts the political establishment as corrupt, inept, and in need of radical change.

The network's reporting often highlights the victimhood narrative - that the "silent majority" is being oppressed by elites, immigrants, and progressives. This form of narrative framing creates a deep sense of grievance, which can be a powerful driver of engagement, especially when tied to stories about immigration, crime, or perceived cultural shifts.

As an example, this network played a key role in boosting Donald Trump's presidential campaign, helping to craft the narrative that Trump was an outsider who could dismantle the political establishment. By continually emphasising the idea that the mainstream media was biassed and untrustworthy, which created a massive following that felt vindicated by Trump's anti-media stance.

These case studies show how misinformation networks don't just spread lies - they create entire worldviews where they construct a narrative in which their followers feel validated and empowered. The goal isn't just to convince someone of a false idea; it's to reshape their reality to such a radical extent that it becomes harder for them to think critically about what they're being told.

Spotting Patterns of Narrative Amplification

The key to seeing through the right-wing pipeline is understanding how narratives are amplified. Here's a checklist to help you spot the patterns of narrative amplification:

1. Look for Over-Simplification. Does the message reduce a complex issue to a simple, emotionally charged soundbite? If something feels too "neat" or "easy," be sceptical.

2. Check for Emotional Triggers. Is the content designed to make you feel angry, afraid, or victimised? Emotional manipulation is a hallmark of narrative amplification.

3. Examine the Source. Who is delivering the message? Are they part of a network that's known for spreading polarising or radical ideas? If it's someone with an agenda, proceed with caution.

4. Trace the Origins. Where did this information come from? Is it a fringe source, or is it backed by reputable outlets? Misinformation often starts in niche, unverified spaces before spreading to mainstream platforms.

5. Look for Repetition. Is the same message being repeated across multiple platforms? Narrative amplification relies heavily on repetition - seeing the same idea from multiple sources makes it seem more credible.

6. Question the "Us vs. Them" Rhetoric. Does the content frame issues in terms of an enemy? If the message is creating a clear divide between "good" and "evil," be wary of polarising rhetoric that's designed to divide.

By keeping these patterns in mind, you can better spot when narratives are being deliberately amplified to manipulate your emotions or reinforce false ideologies. The goal is to pause before reacting and think critically about the content you're consuming.

Doublespeak in Action

Doublespeak is a term popularised by George Orwell in his novel '1984' which refers to the deliberate distortion of language used to deceive, confuse, or manipulate. It's a tactic that has been harnessed by both politicians and advertisers to create a false sense of truth while subtly changing the narrative in a way that serves their interests. By twisting words and phrases, doublespeak allows those in power to present lies as if they were legitimate, and in doing so, undermine the very concept of truth itself.

The Big Lie: How Repetition Makes Lies Seem Real

Orwell's notion of "The Big Lie" isn't just some theoretical concept contained purely in the pages of his novels; it's a practical strategy used by those whose goal is to maintain control over public perception. The core idea behind the Big Lie is simple. The larger and more outlandish the lie, and the more that lie is repeated, the more likely people are to believe it. This is because, when people hear a claim repeated often enough - especially from authority figures - it begins to feel familiar and, eventually, accepted as fact.

For instance, if you think of Napoleon, the historical figure Napoleon Bonaparte, not the dance wizard Napoleon Dynamite. What's the one 'fact' that springs to mind? Probably that he was short, right? Well, that's just not true. He was in fact slightly above average height for his time. But that lie has been repeated so much that many depictions of Napoleon set him as a man of small stature, often with "short man syndrome."

This technique is clearly seen used in politics day in and day out to infuriating levels and plays a big part in the distrust the public have with politicians in general. These repeated falsehoods can range from small issues to extremely impactful ones. Take for instance during the 2016 Brexit referendum campaign, the Vote Leave campaign prominently displayed the claim on buses that "We send the EU £350 million a week. Let's fund our NHS instead."

This claim was repeated in speeches, debates, and advertisements to reinforce the idea that leaving the EU would save money that could be redirected to public services like the NHS, National Health Service. Despite immediate pushback from experts, including the UK Statistics Authority calling it a "clear misuse of official statistics," the figure was consistently used to cement the narrative.

In reality, the £350 million figure ignored the rebate the UK received from the EU and the funding that returned to the UK through various EU programs, making the net contribution significantly lower. But by repeating the falsehood loudly for all to see and hear, the campaign exploited cognitive ease - the psychological tendency for people to believe information they hear frequently.

The result of this repeated lie? Well, this narrative played a key role in convincing voters that Brexit was financially advantageous, framing it as a patriotic act to "take back control," even though the economic realities were far more complex and nuanced.

The Vote Leave campaign could have used more realistic figures and argued the point from a fiscally reasonable standard, but remember the larger and more outlandish the lie, the more likely people are to believe it, and £350 million is a big number that got big reactions.

In this case, repetition transformed falsehoods into "truths" for significant portions of the population. The use of emotionally resonant language - "Let's fund our NHS," - helped obscure the factual inaccuracies, redirecting focus toward feelings of patriotism or injustice. By creating a clear enemy, the EU, the campaign simplified a complex issue into a digestible narrative, even when the foundation was demonstrably false.

Another massively impactful, arguably criminal, case of doublespeak in politics is when The Bush administration repeatedly claimed that Iraq possessed weapons of mass destruction, framing this as a central justification for the 2003 invasion of Iraq.

In this case they often framed uncertainty as certainty with statements like "We know that Iraq has weapons of mass destruction" and "We know where they are" having been made repeatedly in speeches, interviews, and press briefings. Then officials would refer to vague intelligence reports as definitive evidence, avoiding qualifiers like "possibly" or "likely," which would have been more accurate given the inconclusive intelligence.

The Bush administration also frequently linked Iraq's supposed WMD program to al-Qaeda and the 9/11 attacks, despite there being no evidence of collaboration. Phrases like "smoking gun" and "mushroom cloud" were used to invoke fear and urgency, as in Condoleezza Rice's famous statement, "We don't want the smoking gun to be a mushroom cloud." This language deliberately amplified the perceived threat, making it seem immediate and existential.

When asked for proof, officials used doublespeak to deflect, referring to "classified intelligence" or stating that Saddam Hussein's lack of transparency was itself evidence of guilt. This created a circular argument; the absence of evidence became proof of the cover-up. When in reality after the invasion, extensive searches found no evidence of active WMD programs and further to that investigations revealed that intelligence had been exaggerated or cherry-picked to fit the administration's narrative.

The impact of this doublespeak cannot be exaggerated, the WMD claim became the linchpin for public and international support for the Iraq War. Repetition of this falsehood allowed the administration to frame the invasion as a preemptive necessity rather than an act of aggression. The long-term consequences included massive loss of life, destabilisation of the region, and erosion of trust in U.S. intelligence and leadership.

For those of us who lived through those times, the term WMD was used so often that you could repeat those three letters to anyone and they'd still immediately be able to say the entire phrase. A term that would have been vague at best prior to this time.

The consistent repetition of these tactics didn't just mislead the public—it created a narrative so entrenched that it was difficult to challenge even when evidence disproved it. This manipulation of language and information turned public opinion toward a war that many later saw as unjustified.

In Orwell's novel '1984', spoilers ahead, it depicts a world that has been split up into three major alliances, Oceania, Eurasia and Eastasia. With the protagonist living in Oceania. Throughout the beginning of the book it is made clear that Oceania is at war with Eurasia, and has 'always' allied to Eastasia. When suddenly the government propaganda changes and starts repeating "We have always been at war with Eastasia." The characters in this world are so thoroughly brainwashed by the propaganda machine, that only a few seem to question the change in their minds, while everyone else starts to parrot this propaganda. That's exactly what The Big Lie is like.

In today's environment, politicians use doublespeak like it was their native language. You'll see them fall back to carefully constructed slogans and talking points that have been exhaustedly refined through focus groups. Often it's so obvious that it really should be seen as extremely offensive to the general public's levels of education. Especially in a time where video evidence is rife. Politicians will be directly quoted when asked why they've changed their position on a subject, and they'll flat out claim they never said it. It's such a common tactic that news media are now clued on and will often have the exact video from the past of them saying the quote ready to show. In those cases, knowing they've been caught out, politicians will simply move the goalposts to claim that's not what they meant, and immediately try to switch to a slogan or topic that can score points.

As the renowned fashion designer Mugatu once said, "Doesn't anyone notice this? I feel like I'm taking crazy pills!"

Alternative Facts: A Perfect Example of Doublespeak in Action

The phrase "alternative facts" entered the public lexicon during the 2016 Trump administration, when press secretary Kelly-anne Conway used it to defend the false claim about the size of Trump's inaugural crowd. "Alternative facts," as an Orwellian concept, refers to the idea that truth is subjective and can be shaped by whoever has the loudest voice. It's a way of reframing reality, making one version of the truth appear just as valid as another, regardless of the actual evidence.

This is where doublespeak becomes a truly dangerous weapon. It doesn't just mislead people with a false story; it confuses them into thinking that facts themselves can be manipulated or changed at will. It creates a scenario where truth becomes relative, leaving individuals unsure of what's real, what's fiction, and what's just a manipulation of language.

One of the most effective uses of doublespeak in recent political history has been the term "fake news". While the phrase originally referred to deliberately fabricated stories or misinformation, it was quickly co-opted by powerful figures to discredit legitimate journalism. The term was used to label any critical reporting or inconvenient truths as "fake," pushing the narrative that the media itself was the enemy of the people.

By labelling credible sources as "fake" and presenting false narratives as "real news," the term "fake news" became an ideological tool - one that works to undermine trust in institutions and give the appearance of truth to lies.

Doublespeak isn't just limited to politics; it's also rampant in the world of advertising. Consider how companies use terms like "sustainability" and "eco-friendly" to advertise products that are far from environmentally sound. Greenwashing is a prime example of doublespeak in the corporate world, where companies use vague, feel-good language to create an illusion of environmental responsibility, even when their practices remain harmful to the planet.

Take the fossil fuel industry's use of terms like "green energy" to refer to initiatives that are, at best, minimally related to sustainable practices. Or the wildly coined term of "clean coal" as though trying to spin the image of one of the literal filthiest resources, and trying to turn your imagination into thinking of it as some shiny bright diamond. Companies may spend millions on ads touting their environmental initiatives, yet they continue to extract and burn fossil fuels at unsustainable rates. This is doublespeak - language that misleads consumers into believing they're supporting a greener future, while the actions tell a completely different story.

Spotting Doublespeak in the Wild

Doublespeak is a masterful tool of manipulation. Here's your quick guide to spotting it in the wild:

1. Notice contradictions. Does the message contradict the facts? If a claim sounds too good to be true, it probably is - especially when you look deeper into the actions behind the words.

2. Check for emotional appeals. Is the message designed to make you feel something - fear, anger, or righteousness - without offering any concrete evidence? Emotional manipulation is a cornerstone of doublespeak.

3. Repetition is key. If you hear the same phrase over and over again, particularly when it's not backed by any real evidence, be wary. Repetition makes the lie feel familiar and credible.

4. Examine the source. Who is using doublespeak? Often, those in positions of power or authority will use doublespeak to control the narrative. If the person speaking is someone who benefits from the false narrative, question their motives.

Doublespeak is incredibly powerful because it literally warps our perception of reality. It challenges our ability to recognise truth, and when used effectively, it can change the course of entire societies. By learning to spot doublespeak, you can begin to reclaim the truth from those who would distort it.

Aaron Jaeger

Bridging the Divide: The Perception of Elitism

Over the last few decades, one of the most effective tactics used by right-wing media and political figures has been to frame the left as elitist. Whether it's the image of the "liberal elite" in academia, Hollywood, or the tech world, this narrative paints progressive ideas as out-of-touch with everyday working people. The argument goes something like this; Progressives are disconnected from reality, and their policies are designed by out-of-touch intellectuals or coastal elites who live in a bubble, completely unaware of the struggles that real, hard-working people face.

This elitism narrative is so powerful because it plays into a longstanding cultural divide in the United States and other Western countries, the tension between the educated elite and the working class. When political elites on the left talk about policy reform, environmental justice, or economic equality, it often gets framed as an attempt to impose values from the top down without understanding the struggles of the average person. The result? A complete breakdown in communication, and an increasing rift between the two sides.

How the Narrative of Elitism Shapes Perceptions

The narrative of elitism is often rooted in language that reinforces stereotypes. Phrases like "intellectual snobbery," "ivory tower," and "liberal elites" are used to paint progressive thinkers as out of touch with the average person. The right-wing media has a well-oiled machine for portraying left-wing figures, whether they're politicians, academics, or activists, as living in some kind of exclusive bubble that has little to no regard for the struggles of the working-class.

The reality is that many of the people labelled as "elitists" on the left are working to address things like inequality, climate change, and access to healthcare. Yet, the way they communicate their ideas can sometimes inadvertently deepen the divide. Jargon-heavy language, over-intellectualised discussions, and a perceived lack of empathy for people's lived experiences can create an impression that these issues are too complex for ordinary folks to understand, and that's where the elitist tag sticks.

One thing that I'm sure most can agree on is that people don't like to be talked down to, whether you're highly educated or not. If the message being delivered is seen as being condescending then that message will fall on deaf ears.

When we talk about the cultural divide in media representation, one striking contrast emerges, at least from my perspective, which is the tone and presentation of political discourse. Right-wing media often centres its messaging around serious, authoritative pundits who position themselves as thought leaders - think Tucker Carlson or Ben Shapiro. Their delivery is intense, their arguments framed as intellectual, and their tone suggests they're delivering vital truths. In contrast, many of the left's most prominent voices come from the realm of satire and comedy, such as John Oliver, Stephen Colbert or Jon Stewart. These comedians-turned-commentators provide sharp, incisive critiques but often deliver their messages with a punchline.

I think this difference creates a cultural gap in how political messages are received. For viewers and supporters of left-leaning satire, the humour often adds much needed levity to heavy topics, making them more digestible. However, it can also lead to accusations that the left doesn't take things seriously, or again it comes across as Hollywood snobbery. For outsiders of this media bubble, aka those on the right-wing, this tone can feel dismissive, elitist, or even condescending - as if the laughter comes at their expense. And let's face it, it often does.

Think about it, when someone is laughing at you and not with you, it's not a great feeling and your initial reaction will most likely be a defensive one. People do this for the slightest of things, like tripping over a little on the sidewalk. They'll try to pretend it never happened or make bold claims about how it wasn't their fault, instead it was that damned crack in the concrete, the lazy council should really fix that. If someone can be so easily drawn into defensive behaviour over something so common and innocuous, then you can see how jokes made at the expense of their core values are not going to win them over.

Meanwhile, right-wing commentators position themselves as sober truth-tellers, which resonates with audiences craving validation and certainty in an increasingly chaotic world.

The result? A mismatch in how each side perceives the other's sincerity. On the right, the dominance of serious political punditry projects an air of seriousness, reinforcing a perception that their messages are credible and urgent. On the left, comedy-based discourse risks being seen as smug or detached, even when the insights are just as sharp, if not sharper. The cultural divide deepens as humour becomes a barrier to cross-political engagement, with one side laughing while the other side sees a lack of respect.

In this dynamic, satire becomes both a weapon and a liability. It excels at exposing hypocrisy and flaws but struggles to invite those across the aisle into meaningful dialogue. This brand of left-wing comedy often really thrives on an "us vs. them" dynamic, which can inadvertently alienate the very people the left might hope to reach. This framing has allowed right-wing media to accuse the left of looking down on "ordinary people," weaponising the perception of elitism to bolster their own narratives.

So in the end this elitism narrative is particularly damaging in that it undermines the legitimacy of progressive ideas by reducing complex, well-intentioned arguments to the personal flaws of the people advocating for them. If a progressive politician or activist is painted as a "liberal elite," it's much easier to dismiss their ideas, no matter how well-grounded in evidence or morality they may be.

This creates a feedback loop where progressive ideas are framed as elitist, and in turn, working-class communities feel alienated, believing that the people pushing these ideas are more concerned with their own status and power, or poking fun at them, than with addressing their needs.

The Complex Relationship with Education and Class

In the U.S., especially, there's a complicated relationship between education, wealth, and social status. The working class and rural America often view higher education as an institution that is disconnected from their everyday struggles. So when progressives use language rooted in academia or cite complex economic studies to back their policies, the same thing occurs as it does when poking fun at them, it can come off as condescending or unrelatable to people who feel like they're just trying to make ends meet financially.

This view is becoming more widely shared in many western countries and there's a clear generational shift occurring here. Where past generations would have seen value in striving for higher education and knowledge, there has been a slow decay of trust in higher education since the "Boomer" generation.

For generations, higher education was seen as the ultimate ticket to "the good life." It wasn't just a pathway to a better-paying job; it was a promise - a golden handshake from society to say, "Work hard, earn this degree, and the world is yours." For Baby Boomers, this trust in the system made sense. Higher education was affordable - or free, job markets were stable, and a degree often meant a direct line to financial security. College wasn't just accessible; it was a no-brainer investment with guaranteed returns.

But that golden age is long gone. Over the decades, higher education has shifted from being a societal investment to a privatised industry. Tuition costs have skyrocketed, outpacing inflation and wage growth, while public funding for universities has dwindled. College is no longer a safe step in the right direction; it's a financial gamble, often saddling students with tens, or hundreds, of thousands of dollars in debt before they've even started their careers. And for many what's the payoff? Mediocre salaries, precarious gig work, or underemployment. The narrative of "go to school, work hard, and get a good job" has eroded into a hollow promise, leaving many wondering if the system is even worth the risk.

This shift feeds into a broader distrust. If colleges care more about profit margins than preparing students for the real world, why should anyone believe in their worth?

The consequences of this mistrust run deep. Younger generations, particularly Millennials and Gen Z, are increasingly sceptical of the value of a degree. They've seen friends or siblings graduate with honours only to end up working retail jobs while drowning in debt. Meanwhile, the boomers - the last generation to broadly benefit from the old system - often fail to understand why their "back in my day" advice no longer applies. This generational disconnect amplifies the divide. The old mantra of education as a cure-all now feels more like gaslighting to younger workers struggling in an era of stagnating wages, outsourcing, and automation.

What's worse is how this erosion of trust has been weaponised. Politicians and pundits, particularly on the right, have jumped all over this frustration to paint higher education as not just ineffective but outright harmful - a breeding ground for "liberal elitism" or "woke ideology." This rhetoric further undermines the idea of education as a public good, fuelling animosity toward educators and academics while giving legitimacy to anti-intellectual movements. In this climate, it's easy to see why many now view colleges not as gateways to success but as symbols of a system that's left them behind.

These cracks in the foundation of educational trust don't start at college level either; they begin in early education, where rigid systems and underfunding have long left many students behind. Public schools, often strapped for resources, are forced to prioritise standardised testing and adherence to rigid curricula over personalised learning. For kids who struggle to learn in traditional ways - whether due to learning disabilities, personal circumstances, or simply a different pace of cognitive development - this approach can feel like a system designed to fail them.

For these students, the classroom often becomes a place of frustration and humiliation. Instead of being nurtured, they're scolded for not fitting the mould. Instead of finding alternative pathways to success, they're labelled as "problematic" or "lazy." And while these labels might not be spoken aloud, they're often implied in the way the system treats them, not as individuals with potential, but as obstacles to a school's performance metrics. Even to the point that schools will actively try to force out underperforming students, and I know this from lived experience.

At primary school I was close to a "straight A student" and I was accepted into a high school outside of my school zone because my older sister was an overachiever in her academic studies and she attended that same school. So from the first day I stepped through those gates I was let know by the teachers themselves that they had big expectations from me.

I was put into all the top classes and offered guidance and assistance, which at the time I didn't know wasn't a thing that was being offered to others. However, I wasn't much interested in typical academics, I've always been more on the creative side, and I'd constantly be doodling characters in my notebooks and staring out the window daydreaming. Which would in turn get me in trouble, I'd be sent out of the classroom for all sorts of nonsense, and it would drive the teachers crazy when a test would come around where again I'd rank in the top 5 results of my grade.

So the teachers would still constantly stress to me the importance of me paying attention to do better. Outright stating it would help them lift the averages of the school, like a teenage boy raging through puberty cares, right.

I don't say any of this to brag, just previously in this chapter I've been describing the hatred of the educated elite, so I'm sure it's not doing me any good to be talking about 'Oh woe is me' being such a smarty pants. The point I'm getting to is a real life comparison with another student in my grade, with a much different experience.

This student didn't find themselves as keen on studies as I did and they were placed in the lowest classes throughout high school. A major problem being that everyone placed in those lower performing classes, well they weren't exactly strong scholars either. So, in a system that is as rigid as the school system is, these kids were often given the harshest of teachers, they'd of course rebel and get in trouble, they'd miss out on class and in turn fail tests, and the cycle would continue.

In Australia, specifically in New South Wales where I grew up, when you reach the end of the tenth grade, "Year 10," you take an exam called the School Certificate. Once you complete this year of school you can choose to move forward to Year 11 and Year 12 where you complete your High School Certificate and can use that score to move onto University, or you can choose to exit into the real world and get a trade or a job and you're off into adulthood.

So approaching the end of Year 10, I had teachers pushing me to consider what courses I'd do through the following two years and what university I'd go to, encouraging me to think about how much impact these choices would have on the rest of my life. The other student however, had a different story altogether.

One day I just happened to be out doing some task for a teacher, running a note to another teacher or something, and as I was walking between buildings I noticed, under a walkway, the other student was standing there with a couple of teachers who were verbally demeaning them, complaining how if they remained to complete the School Certificate it would have negative effects on the school in general. Mind you this is all to a fifteen year old kid.

On the spot, right then and there, they gave them the choice to turn around, head home and never return to school. They offered that they wouldn't note the student's absence on the record, so as not to alert their parents and that they could simply skip completing the exam. The student's answer was a defiant yes and they turned and walked off, unknowingly toward my direction.

I was shocked, and as the teachers had left, I stepped out from where I had hidden myself and went up to them to try to make sense of what had just happened. I was demanding that 'they can't do that,' trying to convince them to stay and complete the exam in simple protest to the teachers, screw their results and the school. But by that stage they had enough and would rather stick a middle finger up to the teachers, to the school as a whole, and leave, and really who can blame them.

To think, how many millions of children do you think experience that sort of schooling? Where they're consistently left behind and belittled by the educators themselves. It's no wonder, then, that many grow to see educators - and, by extension, education itself - not as allies, but as gatekeepers of an elitist system that never had their best interests at heart.

This resentment can fester for years. When these individuals enter adulthood, they carry the scars of a system that told them they weren't good enough, weren't smart enough, or didn't belong. And in the age of the internet, many might find solace in communities that validate their experiences. These online groups often thrive on rejecting authority, celebrating those who "think for themselves" and deliberately avoid mainstream narratives. It's no accident that many of these communities reject scientific consensus and promote conspiracies like the Flat Earth theory. For those who felt shunned by traditional education, embracing these ideas can become a symbolic middle finger to the system that told them they were always wrong.

But it's not just about validation - it's about power. In these spaces, the very act of rejecting consensus becomes a badge of honour. "Doing your own research" is framed not as a path to truth, but as an act of rebellion against the so-called "elite." The scientific community, the media, and academia - once seen as pillars of knowledge - are recast as villains, accused of manipulating the masses and suppressing dissent. For many, this narrative feels deeply personal. After all, if the system that failed them was built on lies, then rejecting it wholesale feels not only justified but righteous.

This dynamic fuels a dangerous cycle. The more these individuals reject the consensus, the more entrenched they become in echo chambers that reinforce their beliefs. And the more they're ridiculed by those who uphold traditional education and expertise, the more their resentment grows. It's a perfect storm; a population of undereducated individuals who feel empowered by their defiance, validated by their online communities, and alienated from the institutions that could help them find common ground.

Of course, politicians lay in wait for these individuals. For as Orwell himself wrote repeatedly in his book, '1984', as one of the main three slogans central to the Party's propaganda machine, "Ignorance is strength." Which suggests that the ignorance of the masses strengthens the ruling regime. Without the knowledge or ability to question their reality, people are easier to control and less likely to rebel.

Back in our real world, that slogan seems to have become less of a warning of authoritarianism and more of a playbook for politicians to purposefully underfund our education systems, leaving citizens at the mercy of their propaganda.

Breaking this cycle of distrust between the "educated elite" and the "working class" requires compassion and nuance. Ridiculing those who fall into these traps only deepens their mistrust. Instead, we need to reframe education as an inclusive, flexible, and accessible tool for everyone - not a rigid hierarchy that rewards only those who conform. By addressing the failures of early education, creating alternative pathways for learning, and fostering open dialogues with those who feel left behind, we can begin to heal this divide and rebuild trust in the pursuit of knowledge.

Strategies for Reframing Progressive Ideas to Connect with Broader Audiences

To counter the elitism narrative, it's crucial to reframe progressive ideas in ways that resonate with broader audiences - especially those who may feel alienated or disconnected from traditional political discourse. Here are some strategies for reframing:

1. Speak to people's needs, not just the problems. Rather than focusing solely on abstract theories or policy details, connect the conversation to people's day-to-day struggles. Frame progressive ideas in terms of tangible benefits - such as better healthcare, living wages, and environmental protection - that people can directly relate to. These issues are about making life easier and better for everyone, not just about implementing policy for the sake of policy.

2. Use accessible language and avoid jargon. Complex terms and academic jargon can quickly alienate people. When talking about complex issues like healthcare reform, climate change, or economic inequality, try to simplify the language and make it approachable.

3. Acknowledge the concerns of the "other side." Rather than dismissing concerns about taxation, regulations, or government interference, acknowledge that these are legitimate concerns for people who feel that government intervention has hurt their livelihoods. Show empathy for their frustrations and create common ground for discussing how progressive policies can address these concerns without further alienating people.

4. Find common values across political divides. One way to bridge divides is to emphasise shared values. Whether it's

a desire for health and prosperity, security for future generations, or freedom from oppression, these are values that transcend political affiliation. When framing progressive policies, focus on how these values are central to what you're advocating for.

5. Focus on local stories and grassroots movements. Progressive ideas are often best communicated through local stories or grassroots movements that show the practical impact of these ideas in people's everyday lives. Highlight local communities where progressive policies are making a real difference. This brings the message down from the ivory tower and places it directly in the hands of ordinary citizens.

6. Speak from truth, not from jest. As much as we all may need to laugh at the absurdities of our times, in order to keep a shred of sanity. Simply poking fun and "scoring points" or "dunking" on the other side isn't going to win them over to your side. The left needs more voices speaking reason to the masses from a place of truth and understanding and both sides need to be able to concede gracefully when proven wrong and allowed room to move when proved right.

The perception of elitism is one of the biggest challenges to progressive ideas, but it's also one that can be broken down with empathy, clearer communication, and a focus on the issues that truly matter to people. By reframing the conversation, progressives can connect with broader audiences and counter the elitist narrative that often hinders their messages.

Case Studies of Messaging That Successfully Bridged Divides

1. Obama's 2008 Campaign: "Yes We Can"

One of the most remarkable examples of bridging divides through messaging came in Barack Obama's 2008 presidential campaign. Obama's team recognised the deep divisions in America, not just between political parties, but also between socioeconomic groups, races, and education levels. What Obama did so effectively was use messaging that was hopeful, inclusive, and simple. The slogan "Yes We Can" was more than a campaign slogan; it became a unifying message that transcended policy differences and focused on a vision of collective possibility.

Obama was able to tap into people's shared values - such as hope for the future, belief in the power of individuals, and the desire for a fairer, more equal society - without sounding out of touch. He avoided heavy intellectual jargon and stuck with language that anyone, regardless of background, could understand. His rhetoric was rooted in unity, it wasn't about us vs. them, red states vs. blue states. It was about everyone coming together to achieve something greater.

This message resonated across party lines and helped him draw support from working-class voters, minorities, and college-educated professionals alike. Obama didn't just tell people what was wrong with the country; he painted a picture of what could be - together.

2. The "Climate Change is Real" Campaign by Scientists

When scientists and environmental activists began pushing for more aggressive action on climate change, they faced a huge challenge, climate change was (and still is) heavily politicised.

Many right-leaning individuals viewed environmentalism as a liberal cause, and this led to division on the issue.

A breakthrough came when several scientists and advocates shifted their messaging to focus on shared interests, such as economic stability and job creation. Instead of just arguing about the environment, the conversation became about green jobs, renewable energy, and the future of American industry. They reframed the issue of climate change as a matter of national security, economic competitiveness, and health, making it relevant to a broader swath of the population. By connecting climate action to tangible benefits like new industries and job creation, advocates were able to shift the conversation from a partisan issue to a pragmatic, bipartisan solution. With even staunch Republicans like Arnold Schwarzenegger once saying, "I don't give a damn if you believe in climate change. The fact is, moving toward a clean energy future is going to create jobs, reduce pollution, and make our energy system more secure."

These case studies show how powerful the right messaging can be in bridging divides. Whether you're talking about politics, social issues, or even corporate responsibility, the key to changing minds lies in framing the conversation in a way that resonates with common values, real-life concerns, and a shared vision for the future. Unfortunately, we may still have a ways to go on the two subjects of the case studies I've provided, but there's certainly hope when we can continue to successfully bridge the divide.

Part 2: The Tools of the Trade

"The most dangerous propaganda is the one we can't see." - Naomi Klein, The Shock Doctrine

If there's one thing that makes mass deception so dangerous, it's how invisible it often is. The systems that perpetuate lies, misdirection, and manipulation are so deeply woven into the fabric of our society that we rarely notice them at work. They operate behind closed doors, masked by polished narratives and expertly crafted images, subtly shaping our perceptions and beliefs without us even realising it.

These systems are not new. In fact, they've been around for as long as we've had mass media and political power. But what's different today is the scale and sophistication of the deception. The tools used to manipulate public opinion, control the flow of information, and frame reality are now so advanced that they often operate on an unconscious level, influencing our decisions, behaviours, and even our identities.

The truth is, the machinery of deception is vast and complex. It's not just about politicians lying or advertisers using flashy slogans to sell you products. It's about the invisible structures that enable these lies to thrive. From corporate interests shaping public policy to algorithms determining what news you see, the systems we rely on to shape our understanding of the world are often designed to keep us in the dark, distracted, and divided.

In this part of the book, we're going to pull back the curtain and expose these tools. We'll look at the structures - media conglomerates, social media platforms, political lobbying, and corporate propaganda - that manipulate the flow of information. We'll dive into how these systems work together to control narratives, distort truth, and create an environment where deception can flourish unchecked.

The goal here isn't just to identify the problem - it's to understand how these tools operate so that we can start recognising them in our everyday lives. Once we understand the systems at play, we can begin to break free from their grip and take back control of our own understanding of the world.

Traditional Media's Long Shadow

The power of legacy media is hard to overstate. For decades, newspapers, television networks, and radio stations were the gatekeepers of information. The public relied on them for facts, for truth, and for a semblance of unbiased reporting. But as with most things in life, power corrupts - and when profit became the driving force of the media, truth became a secondary concern.

For much of the 20th century, traditional media was dominated by a small number of major players. In the United States, networks like CBS, NBC, and ABC, along with newspapers like The New York Times and The Washington Post, were regarded as authoritative, trusted sources of information. They set the agenda, framed the news, and had significant influence over public opinion. The idea was simple; these institutions had credibility, and the public believed that credibility would always come with a commitment to truth.

But that began to change in the 1980s and 1990s, as media outlets realised that credibility wasn't necessarily what people were seeking. In a capitalist economy, where advertising revenue drives profitability, the news business had to evolve. That's when things like sensationalism, fear-mongering, and the 24/7 news cycle took hold. Suddenly, it wasn't about delivering factual, balanced information - it was about keeping viewers glued to their screens, so they'd stick through the ad breaks and help those media companies to turn a profit.

When CNN first introduced 24-hour news coverage in the 1980s, it felt revolutionary. The idea was to provide constant updates, allowing people to feel informed at all times. But over time, the line between information and entertainment began to blur. Fox News and MSNBC further polarised the landscape by framing news through highly partisan lenses, creating a split reality where the same events were reported in wildly different ways depending on which channel you tuned into.

The result? The rise of media echo chambers, where people seek out information that reinforces their own beliefs, rather than challenging or expanding them. The drive for viewership, ratings, and advertising dollars turned journalism into a competitive, profit-driven industry - where sensational headlines, and emotional manipulation became the order of the day.

This fast tracked the "devolution of truth." The key issue here is the shift from a fact-based journalism model to a ratings-based one. As the 24/7 news cycle took over, traditional media outlets were forced to compete for attention. Stories had to be dramatic, polarising, and attention-grabbing - anything to keep the audience tuned in. The truth, unfortunately, became secondary.

What became important was creating stories that people wanted to watch, not necessarily ones that reflected reality.

Consider how advertisers influence this dynamic. Media companies rely heavily on ad revenue to stay afloat, and advertisers have increasingly demanded media outlets tailor content in ways that keep consumers engaged - and, often, outraged. Sensationalism drives views. Anger and fear keep you glued to your set. And so, over time, the media ecosystem warped into one that prioritised emotional reactions over thoughtful, informative content.

This transformation has eroded the trust that once anchored the relationship between the media and the public. No longer is there a single source of truth; instead, we're flooded with conflicting reports, skewed perspectives, and echo chambers that deepen our divides. As traditional media outlets have increasingly aligned with specific political or ideological viewpoints, they've fractured public trust even further.

The legacy media's long shadow still looms large today. While new platforms like social media, podcasts, and blogs have emerged as alternative sources of information, many people still turn to the big networks for the "truth." The problem is that these outlets often manipulate what truth means, shaping narratives to align with their profit motives and their partisan allegiances.

Now, we live in a world where "truth" is no longer a fixed concept but a commodity to be sold. Legacy media companies continue to operate in this ecosystem, perpetuating a system that encourages divisiveness, reinforces tribalism, and capitalises on conflict. The question is no longer "What's the truth?" but "Which version of the truth do you trust?"

Increasingly since that time, we've also seen the monopolisation of media into just a handful of very large, very powerful, corporately backed entities. So while there may seem to be more choice than ever before, if you follow the breadcrumbs of buyouts and takeovers the pathway often leads you to the same end point.

One of the most glaring examples of how media ownership impacts truth is via one man who controls much of the media landscape in the West. He's also quite litigious so I'll keep his name out of my book. His considerable media empire has an outsized influence on the global narrative with his media outlets having been known to shape political landscapes, particularly in the U.S., UK, and Australia, by pushing agendas that align with his corporate interests and political leanings.

His control of the media isn't just about reporting the news - it's about manufacturing consent. His empire wields the power to define reality, frame issues in a way that benefits his own businesses and political partners, and sway public opinion. The result is a system in which the public's understanding of truth is shaped by a small group of elites, whose primary goal is to increase profits - not necessarily to inform.

This concentration of power is dangerous because it ensures that a single voice or a small group of voices controls the flow of information - creating a skewed, fragmented reality where truth is whatever benefits the people in power.

There are ways to fix this, or at least lessen the impact. As in my home country of Australia it used to be very different. If we rewind time, back to the late 1980s, cross media ownership laws were put in place by the Labor government, Australia's centre left party, designed to strictly prohibit the control of more than one commercial television licence or newspaper or commercial radio licence in the same market, with the idea that the law would reduce the potential for media concentration in the hands of very few elite.

These laws weren't perfect but since they were changed in 2007 by the Liberal party, Australia's conservative party, the media landscape now has an unusually high concentration of media ownership when compared to other western democracies. Allowing for much more control of the narrative, by fewer and fewer powerful interests.

Social Media's New Reality

"The most effective way to destroy people is to deny and obliterate their own understanding of their history." - George Orwell, '1984'

The internet and social media have fundamentally changed how we consume information, but I'm sure most would argue not necessarily for the better. In the past, we trusted traditional media to present the news - often biassed, sometimes sensationalised, but at least with some reliance on professional journalistic integrity and the ability to be fact-checked to some degree. Now, we're living in an age where anyone with a phone and an internet connection can share information - and it's not always truthful.

But the real danger doesn't lie solely in the hands of the public. It's in the algorithms that govern these social media giants, platforms that are powered by a set of invisible rules designed not to serve the truth but to maximise engagement and profit. These algorithms are not in the business of keeping you informed. They are in the business of keeping you hooked. And they've learned a few key tricks from their big brother in traditional media as they do so by prioritising the kinds of content that trigger outrage, emotion, and polarisation.

Prioritising Profit Over Truth

When social media platforms first emerged, they offered a space where anyone could share their voice. Some of us may have naively thought they would be a platform for transparency, dialogue, and the free exchange of ideas. But what's often lost in this utopian view is the fact that these platforms are businesses - businesses that make money by getting clicks and engagement. The more you engage, the more you stay on the platform, the more data they gather on you - and the more space they can sell to advertisers.

To ensure you stick around, social media platforms rely on the all mighty algorithms - complex, data-driven programs designed to serve you content tailored to your interests. These algorithms track your behaviour, what you like, what you comment on, what you share, and how long you spend on each post. The goal? To keep you on the platform for as long as possible, consuming as much content as possible, so they can sell to you as much as possible.

But the issue with these algorithms is that they are not designed to show you the truth. They are designed to show you what will make you engage the most. And what makes people engage the most? Emotionally charged content. Outrage, fear, anger, and division are the primary triggers that compel people to click, comment, and share. Positive content, factual reporting, and calm discourse often gets pushed to the background.

Think about it, when is the last time you commented on something mundane and factual compared to the last time you got drawn into a dumpster fire of a comment section?

The psychology behind why people comment on social media often boils down to a combination of factors tied to human behaviour and the unique dynamics of online interaction. One key reason is anonymity and perceived distance. When people interact online, especially in spaces where their real identities are hidden or not prominently displayed, they experience a phenomenon called the "online disinhibition effect." This psychological effect suggests that anonymity lowers the barriers of social norms and consequences, enabling individuals to express thoughts or emotions they wouldn't normally express in face-to-face interactions.

That lack of non-verbal cues in online interactions plays a huge role in online behaviour. Face-to-face communication is rich with subtle signals - facial expressions, tone, gestures - that help convey intent and emotion. With these being completely absent in text-based comments, it often leads to more misunderstandings and heated confrontations. People may interpret neutral statements as hostile or vice versa, which pours fuel on the fire. And without that immediate feedback of body language or verbal tone, users can end up feeling detached from the social repercussions of their words, making uncivil or extreme behaviour almost the norm online.

If you've ever seen that Key and Peele sketch where two friends are texting each other about catching up, with wildly different perspectives on the tone the messages are being sent in, I'm sure you'll understand and relate.

Finally, social validation plays a significant role. Commenting on social media provides an immediate platform for expressing opinions and receiving attention. This ties into the brain's reward system - likes, replies, and shares provide small dopamine hits that can reinforce certain behaviours, even if those behaviours are negative or aggressive. In polarised or contentious discussions, this drive for validation can push people to make provocative comments simply to garner reactions aka trolls.

In essence, the combination of anonymity, emotional detachment, and the gamification of engagement makes social media a breeding ground for horrible behaviour that people might never exhibit in real-life interactions. Unfortunately though as we move towards a society that has been raised with social media, those interactions and lack of social cues are spilling over into real life more often. Which leads us to a discussion later in this book about how to actually talk to each other free of this one-upmanship.

This negativity bias that all these algorithms have creates a reality where the truth doesn't sell - but rage, controversy, and conspiracy theories do. The owners and CEOs of these platforms have been grilled on this in US Senate enquiries and of course they claim their algorithms aren't specifically built to spread hate, but instead they're only focused on things like engagement. But as we've discussed, hate is a powerful tool in eliciting engagement, so unless we can change our own ways we may be stuck with this cesspit of social media interactions because unfortunately the more extreme the narrative, the more likely it is to go viral. In fact, misinformation spreads faster than facts on social media because it plays to our primal instincts. And that's where things get dangerous.

Control in the Digital Age

When we talk about media ownership in the modern era we really can't look past the owners of these major social media platforms. Their ability to control a much broader, much more complex system, social media, would be the envy of legacy media owners. With only a handful of major players in the field, they hold vast amounts of influence over the flow of information. One of the major shifts being that while traditional media broadcasts to an audience in a one way conversation, social media platforms create an ecosystem where everyone has the ability to be a "broadcaster" and has perpetuated the egocentric view that everyone's opinion not only matters, but is somehow equally as valid. But much like traditional media, the new business of social media thrives when engagement is maximised. And how do you maximise engagement? That's right, you got it. You make sure the content gets people fired up.

The media landscape has undergone a monumental shift with the rise of social media platforms, which have fundamentally reshaped the world of journalism, often to its detriment. Traditional media outlets, once reliant on subscriptions and advertisers for revenue, have been forced to adapt to an online ecosystem where success is measured in clicks and shares. Social media platforms amplify this by prioritising content that drives engagement - usually the most controversial or emotionally charged material - and as a result, journalism has increasingly leaned on clickbait headlines and sensationalism to capture fleeting attention spans, the 24/7 hours news cycle online now forces reaction immediately when any event happens often resulting in journalists skipping past the diligent checks and hours of research they would have done in the days prior to social media, which all in turn is diluting the depth and rigour once expected of news reporting.

This shift has also created a feedback loop of outrage and engagement. Media outlets frequently mine social media platforms for reactions, quoting a handful of extreme posts to frame a story as a widespread controversy with phrases like, "Fans are outraged" or "The internet is divided." These stories then get recirculated back into the feeds, sparking more outrage and engagement, like some demented hellscape version of the circle of life.

With the incessant chase of viral moments, journalism had moved away from focusing on investigative reporting or in-depth analyses, as those stories are costly and take time and resources to report. And when you know most people are not going to make it through a short clickbaity two minute long read, what hope would the media outlets have that they'll follow an intricate story line to the end. That lack of substance in turn for so much spectacle then further erodes the trust the public has for these organisations.

The broader impact is a media environment that thrives on division and short-term engagement rather than fostering informed public discourse. This transformation undermines journalism's role as a pillar of democracy, reducing its capacity to hold power accountable and leaving audiences trapped in echo chambers of outrage-driven content.

Of course, just like traditional media back in its hay day, social media owners now can be king makers, and on an international scale unheard of before, as billions of users login every day. These platforms have helped to foster both good and bad outcomes, depending on your viewpoint. There's been political uprisings that have toppled governments, world health crises that have seen an unprecedented spread of misinformation, and decisions made prior to and post elections that have shaped the outcome of the free world.

We have to ask ourselves, should all this power be kept in the hands of so few?

And it's not just politics and public discourse that suffers. Social media has transformed the advertising industry by offering unparalleled tools for targeting and tracking consumer behaviour. These platforms collect vast amounts of data on their users - ranging from demographics and interests to minute details like scrolling behaviour and watch time. This allows advertisers to deliver hyper-targeted campaigns with remarkable precision, optimising metrics such as click-through rates (CTR) and conversion rates like never before. For businesses, this represents an unprecedented opportunity to reach the right audience at the right time.

However, this precision comes with a stranglehold. The monopoly these platforms hold has created an environment where these companies are the gatekeepers of advertising success. Businesses - both large and small - often have no viable alternatives, as traditional forms of advertising like print, radio, and even television pale in comparison to the measurability and cost-effectiveness of digital ads. Nowadays if you aren't advertising on social media in some way, shape or form, you're effectively invisible to a massive portion of your potential audience.

The power imbalance is stark. Social media platforms not only control the algorithms that dictate how ads are displayed but also set the prices for ad placement. This dominance forces businesses into a system where they must continuously invest in advertising just to maintain visibility, particularly as organic reach has been systematically throttled in favour of paid promotion. As a result, small businesses and startups often face a "pay-to-play" environment that disproportionately benefits those with larger ad budgets.

From a societal perspective, this dynamic consolidates power in the hands of a few tech giants. The reliance on data-driven advertising reinforces consumer dependency on social platforms while also raising ethical concerns about privacy and manipulation. For advertisers, it's a bit of a damned if you do, damned if you don't kind of situation. Social media offers incredible reach and effectiveness, but at the cost of being locked into a system that they really can't afford to escape, or simply have no other option outside of.

The result of all this is that social media becomes a feedback loop of extreme opinions, misinformation, and distorted truths.

People gravitate towards content that reinforces their existing beliefs, and algorithms make sure they never have to confront anything different all in a play to keep feeding you on a steady, and ever increasing, carousel of advertising that often feels invasive and leaves you questioning how much these tech giants are actually tracking you.

Recognising Algorithmic Manipulation

The first step in avoiding the pitfall of algorithmic manipulation is to recognise that social media platforms are not neutral spaces, and they are not "the town square" - they are profit-driven businesses that manipulate the content you see. Here's your checklist for recognising when you're being manipulated:

1. Check the source. Is the story coming from a reliable, fact-based source, or is it from a platform that thrives on sensationalism and outrage?

2. Emotionally charged headlines. Are the headlines designed to make you feel angry, afraid, or shocked? These are often signs of content that is engineered for engagement, not truth.

3. Check the facts. If something seems too extreme, it's probably not true. Look for fact-checkers and independent sources that can verify the claims.

4. Look at the spread. Is the post gaining traction because it's controversial or because it's substantive? Look at the ratio of emotional engagement (likes, comments, shares) versus factual discussion.

5. Do a reverse image search. Fake stories often come with doctored images or videos. Use tools to check whether the media has been manipulated.

By recognising how the algorithms work and being aware of their manipulative tendencies, you can start to take control of your own media consumption and avoid being sucked into the chaos of misinformation.

Visual Lies

"The eye sees only what the mind is prepared to comprehend." - Henri Bergson

In an age where information travels faster than ever before, images and videos have become some of the most powerful tools of persuasion. The saying "a picture is worth a thousand words" has never been more accurate - except, we have to be aware, those thousand words can still be lies.

Visual content is often treated as the most reliable form of evidence. We assume that if we see something with our own eyes - especially in video format - it must be true. After all, how can something be fake if it's right in front of us? The reality, however, is much more complicated. In fact, images and videos have long been used to mislead, manipulate, and misrepresent. Today, these visual lies are more sophisticated than ever, thanks to techniques like selective editing and technology such as artificial intelligence and deepfakes.

While we'll dive deeper into the implications of AI-generated content later, let's start with what we know; visual manipulation is not a new concept. The use of images to frame narratives goes back as far as the earliest days of photography and has only evolved with the advent of video editing, social media, and AI tools.

The Power of Images and Videos in Spreading False Narratives

Imagine you're watching a news story about a protest. You see a video clip of people clashing with police, tear gas floating in the air, and demonstrators throwing objects. The footage seems intense, dramatic, and chaotic - almost as if the entire protest is violent. But what you don't see is the context behind that clip. Was that part of the protest a small minority of the crowd? Was it staged or selectively edited? Was the video doctored?

You see, selective editing is a staple of visual manipulation. A video can be cut, cropped, and framed in such a way that it tells a completely different story than the full picture. In fact, the same footage can be used to push entirely different narratives depending on how it's presented.

For example, in news coverage, a peaceful protest can be framed as a violent mob just by showing the right snippets of footage at the right angles. The framing, the focus on certain people or actions, and the exclusion of others all work together to build the narrative that the media outlet wants to sell. The goal isn't necessarily to tell the truth - it's to elicit the correct response from the viewer.

This is essentially the job of a good photographer or videographer, we're trained on how to use our equipment, angles, lighting, and editing to elicit emotions or to make things look better or worse. Sometimes this is done for mundane purposes or for the simple sake of artistic intent, other times for more nefarious purposes.

Take for example those all too well known infomercials. The ones you get on shopping channels, morning shows and that you'll catch if you're up to late flicking through channels. You know the ones, where the actors are trying to achieve an every day task like stacking some food containers away in the cupboards but are so inept that they end up creating an avalanche of items spilling out of the cupboards and all over the place. I could almost put money on the fact that as you imagine that scene playing out you are seeing the same thing as everyone else on the planet. The colour grade of the shot is dull, often with highly contrasted deep blacks, with the saturation pulled out of the shot so much it's verging on black and white. As the contents spill, the footage is shaky and blurry, the actor perplexed at what to do and a big red X stamps down on screen with that all too familiar buzz sound effect.

This is a trope that surprisingly works really well, that's why it's such a staple. And while you may recognise its use when over done in these over exaggerated infomercials, this same trick is used in all sorts of media. If an advertiser or a news outlet wants to show something in a bad light, they can film it and edit it as subtly or as overtly as they like to play on that narrative.

Picture what Mexico looks like in movies. You know when you actually visit the place that everything is not in yellowish sepia tones right?

Another way you can frame an emotion or feeling is by the literal lens and frame that you're viewing it through. Photographers and videographers are trained in the use of the wide range of lenses available to them and depending on the choice the results of any given image can be widely different.

The old adage of "the camera adds ten pounds" isn't necessarily true, we can choose to add or reduce weight of a subject, by using a telephoto lens or a wide angle lens, taking the image from a higher or lower viewpoint, positioning the light in front, behind, overhead or to the side. So if you've ever looked at professional actors or models and wondered how come you never look that good in a photo, don't worry. Not only do they have teams of makeup artists and extensive post-production editing applied to everything they do, the practical instruments used to capture the image and the talent of the one wielding the camera play a huge role in the end result.

With just these concepts in mind, consider then how easy it is for a media outlet or marketer to present you the story they want you to see.

I spent my time working as a photographer for newspapers, and worked alongside television news rooms and reporters. So I'll tell you what happens; a story comes in via police reports, PR or a journalist might pitch a story from research they've been conducting. The editor in chief or the producer will then assign that story to a team and most importantly, they'll direct them to what story they want to see. Think John Jonah Jameson Jr. shouting out to Peter Parker to get him a damned picture of that spider guy, but this time doing something bad that he can splash across the front page. That's not too far from the truth of how it operates.

So let's say two news outlets send their teams to cover a protest. Outlet number one wants the protestors to look bad, they're searching for a clash with police, looting or rioting. Outlet number two wants the protest to look peaceful and law abiding.

The teams arrive on site and the reality of the protest is that it is rather peaceful, the protestors, only numbering a few dozen, are standing on the opposite side of the road to the police with placards and signs, shouting loudly for the righteousness of their cause. The half a dozen police are simply standing by and ensuring nothing gets out of hand.

For outlet number two, that's not a problem. The photographer pulls out his camera, sets on the wide angle lens, positions himself in the middle of the road and snaps a range of pictures.

The scene presented is one where the protestors are appearing to be far away from the police, as a wide angle lens can exaggerate the true space of a scene, you can see clearly there's not that many of them, and because you can't really see closely, you don't really notice any strong emotion coming from either side. The photographer then takes that image back to the news room, loads them up to his computer and cycles through to find a handful of pictures to present to the editor. He then colour grades the image to be slightly more saturated, bringing out the calming blues of the sky and rich greens of the trees.

For outlet number one however, who have been given the objective to make the protest look violent and out of control. This calm reality is an issue they have to overcome. So instead of a wide angle lens, the photographer pulls out a long telephoto lens aka big zoom lens. He walks around and positions himself behind the line of police officers and zooms in tight over their shoulders. The effect of a long lens can flatten the distance between objects in an image making it appear like the protestors are right up in the face of the police. The photographer looks for a protester who is shouting the slogans of the protest with the most passion, holding the most radical looking sign and fires off a range of photos. He takes those images back to the news room, loads them up to his computer and selects the image that makes the protester look the most angry, he then colour grades the image to enhance the contrast and slightly remove the saturation.

What story do both these two final images tell? And which do you think will cause the most emotional responses when published in the newspaper, on tv and across social media?

As you can see, even with very minimal "doctoring" of the images, without outright lying and photoshopping in things that weren't there. Just the skill of those operating the camera on the ground can have a major impact on how the story is portrayed.

You may think that thanks to smartphones, this sort of fake narrative is more easily exposed than ever before, and while yes in some cases it very much has shone a light on the real story that mainstream media isn't covering, the sober reality is that we're now generations deep into tech savvy everyday people who are themselves very familiar with these techniques and understand how they can shape the narrative by the way they film and edit the content. Making it now harder and harder to sort through what is truth and what is fabricated truths.

Deepfakes and Misleading Visual Content

If selective editing and framing is the "old-school" way of distorting the truth visually, then deepfakes are its terrifying evolution. Deepfakes use AI technology to create hyper-realistic fake videos that are almost indistinguishable from reality. With deepfake technology, it's now possible to make a video look like someone said something they never said, or did something they never did.

In 2018, a video surfaced online that showed President Barack Obama seemingly calling President Donald Trump a "total dipshit." The video was disturbing not because of its content, but because it wasn't real. The video was a deepfake - an AI-generated video that used Obama's likeness and voice to fabricate a message. While the original video was not intended to be a malicious lie, it highlighted just how easy it is to deceive people with realistic content. Today, anyone with access to the right tools can create videos of people doing or saying things that are completely fake, all with no visible disclaimer to show that the video has been altered.

This manipulation of visuals is extremely dangerous because of our inherent trust in the authenticity of images and video. For example, a deepfake could be used to create a video that could damage someone's reputation, sway public opinion, or even influence an election - all without that video being remotely connected to the truth.

So now more than ever we need to have institutions, publications and fact checking authorities that we can all trust in. The argument, at least as I write this, is in full swing about the role either government, media or online platforms should play in fact checking.

Should there be a wild west mentality where everything and anything is allowed, leaving us as the public in charge of assessing what is real and arguing for the truth? Should there be moderation of the content in the form of tagging certain posts and articles by fact checking organisations, especially on social media where misinformation spreads like wildfire? Or should it be removed completely before it gains momentum and who would control such an option?

The debate as I've seen it involves three primary approaches - government regulation, platform self-regulation, and individual responsibility - each with compelling arguments and significant criticisms.

When it comes to handing it over to be a government responsibility there's the argument that governments are currently the ones tasked with protecting public safety and national security, so regulating misinformation kind of fits in with their broader duties. They could implement national laws which can outline clear and consistent rules for the platforms to follow and unlike the platforms themselves the government doesn't have a direct financial interest, or at least we'd hope not, so is less biased from the standpoint of allowing content for financial gain.

However, not every nation is the same. In democratic socialist countries like Sweden, the citizens may have a higher level of trust in their government to act on behalf of their peoples best interests, but certainly in authoritarian nations the restrictions would have a strangle hold over free speech.

Even in countries like the US which regards itself as the beacon of freedom, what level of censorship and suppression of dissent would occur? And let's face it, just because you're an elected official in government, does not mean you're an expert on all topics and often the speed of which policies are implemented would see snails outpacing them. So policymakers would definitely struggle to adapt quickly to the lightning fast digital landscape and depending who is in power, it's easy to see how any party could stifle legitimate discussion under broad definitions of "misinformation."

If you're an advocate for platform self-regulation you could argue that platforms like Meta have the resources and technical expertise to implement systems and functionality to be able to quickly identify and label misinformation. They'd be able to adapt to emerging threats and tailor their responses appropriately or risk alienating their user base due to the ever increasing distrust they'd otherwise face. After all, if they're going to lose traffic to their site and therefore the profits that come with that, surely they would act in accordance to minimise mistrust.

But at this stage of the book if you didn't already have a healthy mistrust of social media platforms, I'm sure you've at very least started to develop one. As we've mentioned a number of times, engagement is the main metric these platforms operate on. So, if harmful or misleading content is driving engagement and they see no financial benefit in curbing it - what's to say they would? Depending also on which platform, the rules may vary and how they apply these rules would differ, as they already do, leading to a deepening of the perception of platform biases when it comes to moderating content, especially in politically charged environments.

Controversies surrounding things like the spread of COVID-19 misinformation really have laid bare the limitations of self-regulation and the conspiracies that then have sprung from that.

The major issue with both above options are the very organisations we'd be asked to hand our trust over to, as the saying goes, 'Power tends to corrupt; absolute power corrupts absolutely.'

So what about taking power into our own hands?

Encouraging individuals to critically evaluate content is certainly what I am aiming to do with this very book by promoting media literacy and resilience against misinformation. Although handing all power over to the whims of the public could also end with what some may say is revolutionary, whilst others may deem it to be catastrophic results.

Also, relying on citizens rather than institutions to determine truth in the hopes of preserving free speech, could see reactionary and retaliatory action taken from parts of the wider community that may feel alienated.

Simply put, many of us lack the skills to identify false information which would allow it to proliferate unchecked, causing more of a rift between groups and individuals would just gravitate towards the content or platform that reinforces their beliefs, compounding misinformation. Which leads us right back to where we are right at this point.

I myself would have to argue for a hybrid approach. Governments, importantly backed by the will of their people, have sovereignty over what baseline standards they wish to uphold, same with any laws or practises within their borders. But unchecked control to remove content or determine themselves what passes for truth, is Orwellian in its purest sense.

Rather, advice should be sought from independent advisory committees as to a set regulatory framework, similar to that of ratings for films and television. This process should occur with complete transparency with debate from the wider community. This approach would not have the ability to be reactionary to each individual case, but it can provide a solid foundation for how platforms and the public can operate.

Platforms then should take on this advice and implement these rules as they see appropriate. Throttling content, as we witnessed especially during the COVID 19 pandemic, saw information being suppressed as platforms implemented algorithms to quickly shutdown dissenting voices outside the official narrative. It's since been revealed that some, not all, of that information might not actually be harmful. Even some of the "wilder" conspiracies that were shared, after further research and information, may have been closer to the official truth than once was thought.

So again, much like with the government, platforms should refrain from being the arbiter of truth. Instead they could implement more fact checking tools which allow for a more studied approach to information, like the ability to quickly reference sources from peer reviewed literature. Having more controls for the public to report misinformation, and importantly require those reports to be backed up with sources.
Essentially, they should be encouraged to transparently reveal the full story in a way that gives fair credit and balance to a subject.

Then lastly, but no less important, individuals need to be educated, from young to old, on how to evaluate content critically and have the ability to quickly source and research fact based arguments.

I liken this trend of garbage journalism that we're all witnessing to poorly written high-school essays. Think about it, if you presented an essay espousing a bunch of wild claims, quoting theories and asserting truths, you'd rightfully be marked very poorly if you provided zero references to source articles or peer reviewed literature. Well, now out in the real world, we are the ones that need to take that critical stance and demand better from media, publications, pundits and platforms.

In the digital age truth does move, but lies move quicker. So let's guard ourselves against these lies and vote with our feet, or engagement in this case. Similar to any business in a free market society, if you don't like it - simply don't go there. If you don't like chocolate - steer clear of Wonka's Chocolate Factory, if you don't like a particular comedian - don't attend their shows, if you don't like a media outlet - don't subscribe or tune in, if you don't like a social media platform - logout.

Questioning Visual Content Effectively

When you encounter visual content - whether it's a news clip, a social media post, or an advertisement - here's a quick checklist to determine if it's trying to manipulate you.

1. Examine the context. Is the video or image taken out of context? Can you find the full video or image to get the full picture?

2. Check the source. Who is posting the content? Is it a credible news outlet, or a source that has a history of

misleading or biassed content?

3. Look for inconsistencies. Does the content look too "perfect" to be real? Deepfakes, for example, often have subtle flaws, such as unnatural facial movements or distorted audio.

4. Question the emotional impact. Is the content designed to trigger an emotional reaction? Does it make you feel angry, fearful, or outraged? These are often signs that it's designed to manipulate you, not inform you.

5. Fact-check. Before accepting a visual as truth, do some research. Use reliable fact-checking websites or search engines to see if the content has been debunked or manipulated.

6. Ask, could this be a deepfake? It may sound paranoid, but with the rise of deepfake technology, it's essential to be sceptical of any video or audio that doesn't come from a reliable source.

Visual content is a weapon in the battle for control over the narrative. It's powerful, immediate, and deeply persuasive. But it can also be dangerously misleading. The ability to critically analyse visual content is more important now than ever before - because the lies are coming at you thick and fast, not just through words, but through the images you see. And in a world where "seeing is believing," this kind of manipulation can be all the more dangerous.

Working for the Machine: Everyday Complicity

"As long as work is an instrument to earn a living and not the expression of a person's faculties, it will remain what it has been since Adam—punishment." - Max Horkheimer, Eclipse of Reason

It's easy to point fingers at the "big bad corporations," the politicians, and the media moguls who seem to control the narrative. But here's the harsh truth; a lot of us are complicit in the system that perpetuates this chaos. No, we're not all running media empires or pulling the strings behind the scenes, but we're still playing our part in maintaining the status quo. We're all part of the machine, whether we realise it or not.

Here's how it works. Capitalism demands that we, as individuals, prioritise survival - and survival often comes at the cost of our ethics. We've all got bills to pay, mouths to feed, and ambitions to fulfil. This financial pressure means that, for many of us, taking a stand against the system feels like a luxury we simply can't afford. And it's not just a personal issue; it's a collective one.

We live in a world that thrives on distraction. Divide-and-conquer tactics are everywhere, designed to make sure that the working class is too busy fighting amongst themselves to challenge the real power structures at play. Think about it, racial tensions, political polarisation, cultural divides, who uses what bathroom - all these issues are heavily magnified by the media and social media platforms because they distract people from the larger, systemic problems. When people are angry about who's kneeling during the anthem or debating which political party is worse, they're not paying attention to the fact that wages haven't kept up with inflation, or that healthcare costs are out of control, or that tax breaks are still being handed out to the ultra-wealthy.

The real problem isn't that you or I are bad people. The problem is that capitalism is designed to keep us distracted and working within the system rather than challenging it. It's a more hustle and grind type of culture than it is a rage against the machine one.

The reality is, most of us are so caught up in the grind of making ends meet that we don't have the time or mental energy to question what's happening in the world around us. Capitalism forces us into a system where we're constantly racing against the clock, scrambling to make more money, keep our jobs, and pay the bills. When that's your main focus, things like ethics, morality, and honesty often take a backseat. It's not that people don't care about these things - it's that they simply don't have the bandwidth to deal with them while juggling all their other responsibilities.

We're too far down Maslow's Hierarchy of Needs to be able to focus on anything but survival.

I've seen this first hand, having been a part of the media industry for the majority of my working life. I entered the industry as a newspaper photographer at just 14 years old, excited that I'd have a chance to use my creative passion as a legitimate career. I was young and naive, I wanted to please the bosses and excel to higher positions within the organisation and larger media workforce. So I was out to prove myself.

As I showed earlier in this book, with how jobs get assigned, a notification would come in and the editor in chief would shout out from the bullpen the names of who would be sent to cover it. I had no real knowledge of the inner workings of the world at that stage, no real strong political or social allegiances, so when the editor said jump, I'd ask how high. If I was told to cover a political event and to paint the politician in a good light, then a flattering image is what they got. We've all seen unflattering images of politicians and it's easier to get them than you might think. Honestly, if you ever try to take a still image of someone speaking at a podium then at minimum 90 out of 100 shots will capture them pulling a silly face, in the midst of blinking or halfway through what looks like them chewing on mid air. So naturally if your editor in chief is after a flattering image, you delete the 90 and keep the 10.

Who am I to choose? I was just a kid, trying to earn enough to get by, seeking the freedom of sustaining my own life on my own pay check.

A couple of years later I began working as a video editor in television advertising. Directors I worked under and other "old dogs" in the industry, camera operators, sound techs, other editors and the likes would often joke about selling their souls to the devil 30 seconds at a time - the general length of a commercial on television. At first I'd laugh along with them, but little by little the devil himself starts to creep into your own soul.

Here I was, a literal cog in the capitalist machine. During some years I was producing over 900 advertisements within the year. Your creativity becomes a spinning wheel, pumping out content. No time for "creative block", no time to question what you're doing when you've barely got time to think during the work hours.

On any given day I might create an ad for a car dealership, a real estate agency, a grocery store, outdoor furniture, hardware or travel insurance. My director would hand me the script, we'd shoot it or have content provided, and I'd get to work. By this stage in life I'm living out in share-houses barely affording to pay rent and live on more than cereal, toast and packet noodles throughout the week. So my goal was simply to do the best job I could, work my way up the ladder and continually increase my wages so I could better my life and my outlook for the future would improve.

This time in the television industry was during what I'd call the downfall of the glory days. The internet had started to boom, sites like YouTube started to pop up, and the strangle hold on the advertising market that TV had once enjoyed unchallenged began to slip away.

So what used to be considered a safe cushy career in media began to fall apart as well. The remote area teams I was working in went from three man production units with director, camera operator and editor, and started to reduce down to just the director and camera op/editor. And eventually at the age of just twenty years old, I took the solo position of director, camera operator and editor for an entire two large regions stretching from Newcastle right up to the border of New South Wales and Queensland, an area half the size of California.

During this whole time, I started to learn how I could have my own little bit of resistance against "the devil". For instance I clearly remember having to create a commercial for a car dealership which was advertising dodgy loans designed specifically to rip off retirees. So I purposefully made the ad look as dodgy as possible, hoping that surely anyone who views that would see it as a scam and avoid it like the plague. I can only hope it saved as many pensioners from falling into the trap as possible.

But again, what resistance can I really have when I'm still focused on keeping myself from ending up homeless?

A funny thing about the film, television and wider industry that I began to see is that the majority of the workers were very left leaning in their world view, often an industry that was filled with outcasts and people who would enjoy recreational substances in their spare time, at least amongst the creative types. The "us vs them" attitude was often seen between the creatives and salespeople or managerial positions who were generally more "rah rah" about capitalist values, chasing down more clients, bigger budgets, more revenue. While us creatives would plod along and put our skills to use where we were told.

So it used to leave me perplexed when I'd see so many hard right wing media shows. I'd often wonder, who are the people standing behind the scenes here? Are they filming some crazy dude screaming about water turning the frogs gay, then heading home to smoke weed in the evenings and listen to Bob Dylan, while contemplating the complexities of life? While I don't doubt there's a fair share of creatives who may hold these right wing views, it really struck me when, as life progressed, and I had a wife and kids to take care of, I myself would be faced with the decision of holding up my morals and values vs accepting the money and keeping food on the table and the lights on for my family.

In the end capitalism uses the carrot and stick technique, which is a powerful tool to keep people compliant. On the surface, it seems like we have plenty of options, like there is the possibility of one day reaching the carrot, but when you dig a little deeper, you realise that the vast majority of capitalism is just hitting you with a stick, keeping you aware that you must comply or lose it all. This illusion of freedom is part of the deception that keeps us in line.

If we're always struggling to survive and constantly distracted by trivial issues, how can we ever challenge the bigger questions, like why are we constantly fed misinformation? Or how do we start the revolution to a better system?

For example, consider the media companies that thrive off of clickbait content and outrage-driven narratives. The people creating these stories aren't necessarily evil - they're under pressure to get clicks, to get ratings, to make a living. They might even believe, on some level, that they're doing a public service. But at the end of the day, their job is to feed the machine, not expose it. Their pay check comes from feeding that same system of lies, sensationalism, and division.

The divide-and-conquer strategy isn't just something that happens in the boardrooms of major corporations; it's something that keeps us fighting amongst ourselves. When people are distracted by culture wars, polarising political debates, and social issues, they're not focusing on real systemic change. These distractions are incredibly effective because they keep us from looking at the underlying issues - like economic inequality, poor working conditions, and the power of corporations.

Take the media's obsession with things like cancel culture or the "war on Christmas." The media hypes up these issues, knowing that they'll get people talking, sharing, and arguing online. It's easy to get caught up in these debates, especially when they're framed as being about freedom of speech, identity, or values. But when we focus too much on these smaller issues, we lose sight of the fact that the real battle is happening in the economic system - where corporations control more wealth than entire countries, where workers are still struggling to make a living wage, and where the working class continues to get left behind.

By pushing the narrative of us vs. them, the powers that be can keep the working class at odds. Meanwhile, the people at the top keep getting richer, and the cycle of distraction and division continues.

It's a cycle that's hard to escape from - so if you are in it and you feel trapped, know that you're not alone and that we can take steps to make that change towards a better future. We can collectivise and create a media, political and online environment built around higher ideals.

Identifying Complicity and Making Ethical Career Choices

We may not all be working for Murdoch or Zuckerberg, but that doesn't mean we're not contributing to the system that perpetuates the deception. It's important to recognise when you're part of the problem and when you're being complicit in something you don't believe in.

Here's a quick checklist to help you identify whether you're unknowingly supporting a deceptive system:

1. Are you contributing to the status quo? If your work relies on creating distraction, sensationalism, or misleading narratives, it's time to reconsider your role.

2. Are you prioritising profit over truth? If you're in a job where your pay check depends on selling lies, ask yourself if it's worth it in the long run.

3. Are you enabling division? If your work is contributing to the divide-and-conquer tactics that keep people distracted, start thinking about how you can change your approach.

4. Are you in a position to make a change? If you can influence how content is created, how products are marketed, or how policies are shaped, it might just be time to do so ethically.

Remember, making ethical career choices is about more than just choosing the right job; it's about recognising your role in the broader system and deciding whether you want to be part of the problem or part of the solution.

And if you're not in a role that can directly affect the way these systems work from the inside, you can still make change with the choices you make and where you choose to place your attention and your all mighty dollar. Support ethical businesses, shop local or with co-ops, tune into news and media that is delivered in line with facts and ethics, and engage in positive posts and social media.

Capitalism might be built on a system of exploitation, but we can choose to take a step back and evaluate whether we're complicit in the deception. The choice is always yours, but it starts with recognising your role in the machine.

Part 3: Becoming Media Literate

"The most valuable thing in life is the ability to think for oneself." - Marcus Aurelius

If there's one skill that can protect you from the chaos of modern media, it's the ability to think critically. In a world where information is weaponised to manipulate, deceive, and divide, it's no longer enough to passively consume the content being thrown at you. To navigate the noise and find truth, you need to cultivate media literacy - an essential skill that empowers you to evaluate, question, and dissect the messages coming your way.

In this part, we'll explore how to sharpen your mind and arm yourself with the tools to critically analyse media. We'll tackle the strategies that can help you spot bias, identify misinformation, and develop the judgement to separate fact from fiction. It's about reclaiming your intellectual autonomy and learning to think independently in an age where the truth is often buried beneath layers of noise.

By the end of this part, you'll have a toolkit to not just survive the media landscape, but to thrive in it. You'll learn how to challenge the narratives being pushed on you, and how to identify when you're being manipulated. It's time to stop being a passive consumer of information and start being an active participant in the quest for truth.

The Three Horsemen of Manipulation

Alright, let's get real for a second. You've seen it. The outrageous headlines, the cherry-picked quotes, the "facts" that don't quite sit right. But here's the thing, media manipulation is everywhere. It's not just happening on conspiracy websites or shady social media posts - it's happening on the front pages of your major news outlets too. And if you don't learn to spot the patterns, you'll keep getting played.

The truth is, the media - yes, especially the big-name outlets - have been perfecting the art of manipulation for decades. It's not just about informing you anymore; it's about getting clicks, views, subscribers, and - let's face it - ad dollars. The pattern? It's simple. Headlines grab attention, content bends the narrative, and visuals seal the deal.

1. Headlines:

These are the bait.

The goal isn't to tell you what happened, it's to get you to click, pick up the rag or stay tuned. Ever notice how the headline is often sensational, misleading, or completely divorced from the story's actual content? That's not an accident. Headlines are crafted to provoke emotion, whether it's outrage, fear, or curiosity. They want you to react, not think. If a headline feels extreme, chances are, it probably is.

A great example of this comes from legacy media, specifically television news. They'll often leave you with "cliffhanger headlines". You probably have heard the phrase "cliffhanger" before in reference to episodic television. We've all seen it and been suckered into it, it's only natural. Let's say you're watching your favourite one hour drama show, you're hooked deep into the story and hardly notice time going by, suddenly it builds up where the main character is about to do something incredible, they're about to uncover the secret, reveal the truth and...credits roll. That's a cliffhanger, you have to see the next episode to find out more.

You can really notice it now in the modern days of streaming, if you watch a show that was originally produced for 90's television. In some of these shows, you'll clearly see the build up to the cliffhanger moment, then without cut they repeat the exact same scene. You might be left wondering if you accidentally sat on the controller and skipped back a minute or two, but no, that's just where the ad break would have normally been.

Just like they do in shows, if there's ad breaks in news they know that the goal is to try to keep you tuned in through their sponsors because that's who's paying their bills. They might have three to five minutes of pillow ads, prescription drug commercials and fast food deals for you to have to sit through, if they don't place a cliffhanger headline to keep you tuned in, you may just decide to switch channels, or heaven forbid turn off the television and engage in some other real world activity. So you'll often see world ending fearful headlines right before the break, which are there by design to make you feel like you must stay and be informed!

When it comes to social media, they've been able to take the historical learnings from the legacy media and incorporate that into their feeds in a far more effective way that plays on providing you with those hits of dopamine and adrenaline, using similar tactics to those of gambling to keep you hooked. They even use addict type language in describing their customers as "active users."

Newspapers in real world scenarios use big bold attention grabbing headlines because they need to capture your attention out there amongst all the craziness of the world. If you're in a train station and you notice a headline which reads that 'WW3 HAS BEGUN', it's surely going to spark your interest. The outlets know you won't be able to just pick it up and read it at the news stand, the staff will quickly ask you to pay for it. So the editors make sure the few brief paragraphs on the front page give you just enough tantalising details to leave you needing to read further into the paper. Then with that headline story sitting on page 5 you'll be forced to flick through a few pages featuring rather bold in your face advertisements before you get to the main story.

That's the exact theory that social media began with, but the way they can target your specific interest, monitor exactly when you stopped scrolling, when you engage and don't mean they can continue to feed that same, or similar, topic to you and keep you "active".

2. Content:

Now that you're hooked, it's time for the content to do its thing.

This is now where the organisation that made the post really gets to drive their own revenue, shared of course with the social media platforms. So you'd be fooled to think you're going to get anything of substance right up the top of the article. They'll bury it deep down the bottom of the page so you're forced to scroll past dozens of ads before you actually get all the information - that is if they choose to present you with all the information.

Take for example a post I myself saw just recently. A huge boxing match had just taken place between Mike Tyson and Jake Paul. It was one of the most viewed boxing matches in history, and there was a lot of drama and speculation surrounding it. So of course news platforms were scrambling to create as much content from the fight as possible and with a heated debate post fight about whether it was rigged or not, they knew they could drive engagement by fuelling that fire.

The headline read, "Tyson and Paul Suspended After Boxing Match". With all the talk about the fight being rigged, that's intriguing and either side of the argument would jump to see what that was about. Within the article itself, each short paragraph was spaced with an advertisement in between, with pop ups to sign up to this or that occurring every few scrolls. Until right at the very bottom it finally revealed the details about the attention grabbing headline. The big reveal, after all that? Both boxers must officially take x amount of days to rest before entering another sanctioned fight. Which is absolutely standard practice. But that was enough to earn the clicks and fuel the engagement with what was going on in the comments section I could only describe as being a festering pile of garbage.

You might view that example as just business and usual, similar to trying to read a recipe on any food blog, you know you'll have to scroll through the author's life story before you get to the 2 minute recipe at the bottom of the page.

However with the content you also have to be aware of more insidious tactics, like how the language is framed. When you read the article, you need to read between the lines, pay attention to what's left out. Often, what's not said is more telling than what is. For there are countless examples where the media will cherry pick one line out of a complex scientific study and use that to justify their own standpoint, which if you read the published paper from which they've extracted that line you find out that the experts behind the study were pointing to a completely different result than what the media was trying to tell you.

Basing an entire media circus off "ocean levels aren't rising," is vastly different if the rest of that sentence ends in "at levels previously predicted, it's much worse."

You also need to look for loaded words that shape your feelings. Phrases like "experts warn," "sources say," or "scientists agree" are used to lend authority to claims often without actually explaining the why or how. How many times have you seen a movie reviewed with "audiences agree", to then find out that the article has pulled two quotes from random people online to justify that claim. Which brings me to a point which we'll dive into deeper below about how to find reputable sources.

3. Visuals:

This is where the media plays dirty. As we've spoken about previously in this book, images and videos are often selectively edited or chosen to enhance the emotional response they want from you. Think of a news story about a protest. The one with a dramatic close-up of a burning flag is more likely to be shared than the one with people calmly talking about their grievances. Visuals carry immense weight in how we process information, and they're often used to manipulate the narrative more than you might realise.

There is a level of solace that I take here in the modern generation's ability to distinguish visual trickery. When I began in the world of photography, everything was done on film, so it was an expensive hobby just to take still images. Let alone with video, where you'd have to be able to afford tapes or actual film reels, then the mass of equipment needed to process and edit all that film.

Nowadays, everyone has a phone in their pocket with the ability to take incredible pictures and videos. So the skill of how to use lighting, angles and framing isn't an unknown art form to much of the younger population. So you have a level of questioning, from a standpoint of decent knowledge that is happening now unlike ever before.

A prime example of this has been with aliens and UFO footage. Like in 2024 when an incident occurred at a Miami Mall, where there was said to be around 60 police cars turning up, and the narrative spread quickly that it was because there were reports of aliens inside the mall. To this day, at least at the time I'm writing this, there has been no confirmation of what actually happened that has satisfied the majority of everyday people. But one thing that is commented often is, "Where's the footage?". They mean to tell us that hundreds of people were in the mall and the only footage of these supposed aliens comes from what seems to be a shaky handheld potato?

This similar theme happens a lot now with alien footage, where people immediately will become suspicious of the footage itself if it's not "caught in 4K".

I'm not here to start arguments over if aliens are real or not, the US Government certainly has been sharing a lot of hearings lately "confirming" existence of UAP's and the like but again the argument for a lot of the public circles back to "show us". Because we have become so much more adept at seeing visual trickery, that unless it's confirmed in 4K we don't care.

This level of healthy scepticism bodes well for when it comes to all stories and all forms of media that are presented to us as "truth". Especially as we move further into the world of AI.

Finding Reputable Sources

Now that you know the tactics, let's talk about how to avoid getting sucked in.

Reputable sources exist, but they're not always easy to find. And there's rightfully been a loss in trust for mainstream media sources, even traditionally respected sources with a track record of factual reporting such as The New York Times, BBC, The Wall Street Journal, or The Guardian have their fair share of misleading reporting, because in general the more popular the source, the more likely it's being shaped by external pressures like advertisers, political interests, or outright sensationalism.

One of the major issues with traditional media is that, well, it's been dying a slow death ever since the launch of Google and the rise of social media. Previously, they didn't have to worry so much about losing sponsors and advertisers because, simply put, there was no other choice.

Yet now when even the biggest outlets are faced with closure if their ad revenue slips for more than a couple of quarters, the power has shifted back to the corporations that are paying for the ad space. So are you going to release a damning report on the effects of sugar in drinks, if the cola giants are bankrolling your entire payroll? Probably not right.

So, in finding reputable sources start by diversifying those sources and checking multiple perspectives. No one outlet or platform should be your sole source of truth. Then if you want to know what might be behind their views on any particular topic, check the "About" section on their website for transparency about their mission, funding, and ownership. Reputable outlets clearly outline these details for the world to see. If that information is buried or not shown, it's a sign to take everything with a dose of scepticism.

If the information is clearly displayed, there still might be conflicts of interests but you can at least judge their content and articles with a healthy understanding of where that interest comes from.

In today's media environment you'll find that often opinion pieces are given the same weight of gravitas as fact-based and thoroughly research journalism. It's important then to always check where the article, segment or video fits within that range?

A common tactic on modern news media will be to have those "talking head" segments, where they'll invite multiple people via video call or to sit around a table to comment on a given topic or series of questions. The so-called "experts" in these segments can range from Nobel prize winning experts, to social media influencers, all presented on the one screen and treated as though their opinions are equally as valid, which is clearly absurd.

This tactic has held back the discussion on many important topics that have a scientific consensus, like climate change. Where 97% of climate scientists agree that humans are causing climate change. So there is an inherent falsehood in presenting one climate scientist debating one denier, which gives an impression of a 50/50 split on the argument. Where in reality a fair view on the argument would be to have 97 climate scientists arguing for and only 3 against.

Therefore whether the information is being delivered by a solo pundit, presenter, reporter or author, or a collection of "experts", you really need to check and be aware of the person's credentials, expertise, and affiliations. If the Marlboro man himself is arguing that smoking is good for your health - which isn't far from what happened in the past - you should indeed be very wary.

A great way to quickly understand if a subject is being presented fairly is to scrutinise the content for how biassed or balanced it is. Be cautious of sources that present only one side of an argument as often a balanced article will acknowledge counter arguments and be able to refute that alternate view. For really, if you're in the right, you have no need to be worried about shedding light on what is wrong and debating it fairly.

Factual arguments also generally refrain from being overly sensationalist and more often than not they'll be able to maintain a neutral tone, especially when it comes to personal attacks, as drumming up overly emotional language can signal a lack of objectivity and if you must result in attacking the person and not the issue then you've not got a solid enough argument to stand on its own.

Of course there is room for passion in sincerity and depending on the subject there may be an actual cause for alarm, I would certainly still trust a firefighter if they were passionately yelling at me to escape a burning building.

A major area in which modern day media practices has failed the general population is when it comes to citing sources. I mentioned before in this book that if you were to write an essay in high school and omit all your sources, you'd be fairly marked low. So perhaps this is something that should be more regimentally taught and practised in our schools but in any case we are here now and we must learn to routinely check for where the media has gathered their information. Do they cite studies, reports, or other sources to support their claims? Then check the quality of those references.

When it comes to scientific studies, the very basis of the scientific method has rigorous peer-reviewed systems built into it. Academic journals that feature peer-reviewed studies are vetted by experts and the scientific community as a whole, and you don't have to be part of a university to access this knowledge. A little known resource here is Google Scholar which provides access to academic articles that you can read freely.

I would always encourage a healthy dose of, I wouldn't call it scepticism in this case but maybe intrigue would suit better, so a healthy dose of intrigue whenever you see articles written or media talking about, "a recent study suggests," or "a new study finds," because a lot of time, even though to be placed in the scientific journal it would have been peer reviewed, the findings or hypothesis may not have yet been widely accepted in the scientific community. But those who are reporting on scientific issues, are just like all media and scrambling to continually feed the beast, so they'll report on fringe scientific findings before full scrutiny has taken place. So if you see a wild science claim, keep your eye on the space and see how it plays out over time.

Speaking of fact-checking, there's obviously independent fact-checking organisations such as PolitiFact, FactCheck.org, or Snopes to verify claims. Fact-checkers assess the accuracy of statements made in the media and by public figures and they'll often outline why the way that issue was presented was correct or misleading. They'll cite sources themselves and provide a solid guide for quick reference.

I'd always recommend not to take this information at face value either by cross referencing these sites themselves and viewing alternate resources. Be very wary however if you can only find a single source to any claim, especially if they seem sensational, because if only one outlet is reporting on it, it's a good sign that it's not credible enough for others.

Of course you also want to understand who owns the publications, websites, networks or platforms and consider the biases those owners may hold and how they may influence how issues are framed. A glowing article in the Washington Post about Amazon working conditions should be viewed with an overly healthy dollop of scepticism.

I know there's a lot to consider in this section of the book, so let's bring it all back to some simple practical application that you can put into use as of today, in a short checklist.

When presented with a media narrative, ask yourself:

1. Who's behind the source? Look into the organisation's history, ownership, and funding. If you see ties to corporations, political parties, or financial interests, be extra cautious.

2. What's their track record? Does the source have a history of accuracy, or do they regularly get things wrong?

3. What are they leaving out? Pay attention to omissions. Are they presenting the whole picture, or just a cherry-picked sliver?

4. Who are their experts? Are they quoting credible, relevant authorities? Or are they using nameless, faceless "experts" whose credentials can't be verified?

5. Does it feel sensational? Headlines, language, or visuals - are they designed to make you feel something strong (anger, fear, outrage)?

6. What's missing? Are key pieces of information or context left out of the narrative?

7. Can I verify the facts? Cross-check the story with other reputable sources. If you can't verify it, it might not be true.

That's how you start training your mind to spot manipulation and deception in the media. It's about being aware of the patterns and asking yourself the right questions. But here's the thing, the more you practise this, the easier it becomes to spot the bullshit. And the more you can spot it, the more you can avoid getting played by it.

Breaking the Echo Chamber

We've all been there. You click on a link, read a few articles, and before you know it, you're deep into a rabbit hole. The same ideas, the same talking points, the same people agreeing with you, reinforcing your beliefs over and over. And at first, it feels comforting. You feel like you're right. The outside world is full of idiots, and finally, you've found a corner of this crazy world where people get it.

But here's the hard truth, it's a psychological trap, and it's designed to keep you trapped.

Social media algorithms and biassed media outlets know that outrage is a hell of a drug. So they keep feeding you content that confirms what you already think and feel, ensuring you stay in that feedback loop of self-righteousness and division. The more you consume, the more entrenched you become. The more you hear that everyone who doesn't think like you is the enemy, the more you start to believe it.

And guess what? The media loves it. They get the clicks, views, and ad revenue. You get a confirmation bias that reinforces your existing worldview, it's a win-win right? Unfortunately the real loser here is society - and you - because when you're stuck in an echo chamber, you're not just becoming more disconnected from people who don't think like you, you're also becoming less capable of seeing the bigger picture.

It's obvious right? Echo chambers form when you stop engaging with diverse perspectives and you've probably even trashed talked the other side as being in an echo chamber, which if you've had the confidence to voice that opinion might just mean you're in one yourself.

The pathway into this state starts subtly, with a few articles that agree with what you already think. You share them, and your friends who think like you share them too. Then, more content gets recommended that feeds into those beliefs, and before long, you're only consuming a narrow slice of the world's ideas.

Here's the kicker, this isn't just a political thing. You can start falling into many different echo chambers, dog people vs cat people, paleo diet vs vegetarian, atheist vs religious, or the ever so heated family bond shattered argument of whether pineapple belongs on pizza. If you ever find yourself having fallen into an echo chamber and you catch yourself having very dramatic and polarised views on the opposing side, that should be your warning sign to take a beat and really evaluate where your stance has come from and the validity of your opinions.

When it comes to politics, it can happen on both sides of the aisle. Conservatives and liberals alike fall into these traps. The left might build their echo chamber around progressive politics and socialist change, while the right might lock themselves into conservative, neoliberal, or even extremist views. But it's the same cycle. We're all guilty of it at some point, I've certainly found myself guilty of this numerous times in my life.

It happens because the brain loves comfort. It loves certainty. And when we surround ourselves with ideas that already align with our views, we get that sweet, sweet hit of dopamine. We feel validated, like we're "right." The problem is, comfort doesn't create growth. If you're only listening to people who think like you, how are you ever going to challenge your assumptions or even find common ground with those who see things differently?

I can attest to this myself, as I was raised in small town Australia which, whilst it wasn't an official policy of the country anymore, still was very much in the hangover of the old "White Australia

Policy". At my school, in a grade of a couple of hundred students, the amount of non-white kids could be counted almost on a single hand. The town itself was far from the multicultural melting pot you might find in larger cities like Sydney and Melbourne, and if you wanted takeaway food you had the option of Pizza Hut, McDonalds, KFC, Fish and Chips and the one Chinese restaurant, it was big news when the first Thai restaurant opened...how exotic. So hardly a beacon of cultural diversity for the taste buds.

Things did improve as I grew older, but fortunately for myself I was always interested in travel and discovering other cultures thanks to the influence of a couple of travelling Aunties who would always tell me tales of their adventures overseas.

Obviously I didn't grow up in the 1700's either so I was able to see the world on screen, but it wasn't until I had the opportunity to travel overseas myself that my eyes were truly opened to the enormity of the world around me. To be fair I didn't exactly throw myself into the great unknown either, with my earliest solo travels being to Canada, UK and Europe, so I wasn't exactly standing out from the crowd and the cultural changes were not extremely confronting. Yet as I'd people watch in all the places I visited, the simply the understanding that all these lives are being led on the complete opposite side of the world to where my whole existence had been was a mind altering experience. It's one thing to understand it theoretically, another to experience it.

It was landing in Dubai though that truly hit me like a ton of bricks. As that was the first time I had felt like I was, as a white person, not in the majority. There's those of you who might be rightfully laughing at the thought that Dubai was a culture shock, for while yes the locals certainly dress differently and have different customs, being of course a Muslim country, the city as a whole is quite accommodating to westerners and our values.

Why does this all matter in breaking the echo chamber? Ok, I'll get to the point. During my time there I had the opportunity to talk with locals, to partake in their customs and to have some really beautiful and memorable moments. I had grown up as a millennial who witnessed 9/11 and all the craziness that followed, yet I really had very little understanding of islamic culture and its practices. When I returned to Australia it was during a time where the debate was raging in the media and in the community around Muslim women being able to wear their religious head coverings, like the hijab, niqab and especially the burka.

I found myself stunned by how that conversation had been framed and how people I loved were echoing the talking points being blasted across the media. I had spent close to nine months travelling the world and not consuming any news media, just living and experiencing the different cultures and people I met along the way and then here I was, feeling like I had just been outside of some weird little bubble for so long that the argument and the way the debate was being carried out seemed all just so... silly.

That's what you'll find when you break outside of your echo chamber. Sure you may be confronted with arguments that are against your belief system, and they may still remain that way even when you've been presented with the best the other side has to offer. But if you approach life with the pure goal to gain further knowledge and understanding, if you can do away with your ego and approach an idea from another perspective. That's where you'll find your true self, and generally where you'll find that most people are not that different from you.

We may all develop different values throughout our experiences in life, but at a base level, most people are kind. At the very least they're not setting out to be the villain of the story. Most people are seeking belonging, love and friendship. They strive for a life that provides a sense of security, with food in their bellies and a roof over their head.

Remember, we are not each other's enemy. The "us vs them" narrative is only beneficial to the top elite class who want to keep us distracted on silly little arguments so that we don't question the larger truths. So don't buy into the media and the algorithms bullshit, which makes us think we're worlds apart, the truth is, we're all on the same planet trying to figure out how to make sense of this crazy universe.

So, what are some steps to break free from the echo chamber?

1. Stop avoiding discomfort. Engage with ideas that make you uncomfortable. Yes, I know - it sucks. But it's necessary. When you only hear ideas that reinforce your own, you're not growing. Pick up articles, podcasts, or YouTube channels that you wouldn't normally listen to. Challenge your assumptions. If you're left-wing, check out conservative perspectives. If you're right-wing, listen to liberals. You might not change your mind, but you'll understand where they're coming from - and that's powerful.

2. Diversify your media sources. Don't get all your news from one outlet. Diversify. Follow a range of sources, not just the ones that feed your bias. Balance is key - you don't have to agree with everything you consume, but you do need a broader view of the world. Look for independent journalism, foreign perspectives, and fact-checking sites. You want a balanced intake of information, not an echo of your own voice.

3. Stop demonising the "other side." The people you disagree with aren't your enemy. They're humans with different experiences, beliefs, and backgrounds. We can agree to

disagree without seeing each other as threats. This is the crux of breaking the echo chamber, recognise that you're all in this together. If we stop seeing opposing views as personal attacks, we open the door to genuine conversations, better understanding, and maybe even common ground.

Breaking the echo chamber isn't easy. It's uncomfortable, it's messy, and it's painful. But it's also one of the most important things you can do to start seeing the world as it really is - not as the media tells you it is.

Building Truth-Based Communities

You've been told that truth is hard to come by, that it's hidden in a sea of lies, misinformation, and half-truths. And yeah, sometimes it feels like we're all swimming in the deep end of the bullshit pool, trying to figure out which way is up.

But here's the thing, truth doesn't just exist in isolated facts or obscure studies - it exists in communities. In conversations. In collective effort. It's not just about what we know as individuals; it's about what we can discover together when we take action, share resources, and make informed choices as a group. That is the strength we have as humanity.

And no, I'm not talking about some utopian dreamland where everyone agrees on everything. What I'm talking about is communities - whether online or offline - that are dedicated to seeking truth, fact-checking the narrative, and holding each other accountable. Communities that don't just accept information at face value but actively challenge it, verify it, and spread it responsibly.

It's easier to feel like the world is full of lies when you're alone. But the beauty of community is that when we work together, we can push back against the narrative built by corporate media, influencers, and algorithmic manipulation. That's how you fight misinformation - not just as an individual, but as a collective.

Building truth-based communities starts with the recognition that we, as individuals, don't always have all the answers. And that's okay. But we need to encourage critical thinking as a central value in every conversation, every debate, and every piece of information we consume.

Critical thinking isn't just about "dissecting" what's said. It's about recognising bias, understanding the context, and questioning sources. It's about being uncomfortable with easy answers, and pushing ourselves to ask the deeper questions. For example, a headline may scream "BREAKING NEWS: Scandalous Political Move!" But before we share it or comment on it, we need to stop and ask, Is this the full picture? Who benefits from me believing this?

By developing these communities - whether they're discussion groups, local meet-ups, or activist coalitions - they'll help create an environment where critical thinking thrives. When we surround ourselves with others who are dedicated to seeking out the truth, we become sharper. We see more angles. We challenge each other, and we get better at seeing through the smokescreen of manipulation.

But this movement doesn't just happen online.

One of the most powerful ways to combat misinformation is to take it offline. Yes, the internet is great for research, sharing articles, and spreading information, but if we're going to create change, we need to be active in the physical world. Think about it - how many times have you seen a well-meaning post on social media that said, "Everyone should do X, Y, and Z," but then nothing changed in the real world? For those old enough, Kony 2012 springs to mind. People get comfortable online because it feels like they're doing something, when in reality, that post was a drop in the ocean.

The truth is, change doesn't only come from memes or retweets. It comes from in-person conversations, community-driven actions, and grassroots movements.

Real-world activism can be as simple as starting a local book club to discuss media literacy, perhaps with a focus on real world issues and not fictional stories. You could hold a non-confrontational, open debate about politics at your local café or university. It's about creating spaces where people can ask questions, have discussions, and, most importantly, challenge the narratives that they've been sold.

The best part? It's not about fighting anyone. It's about bringing people together to learn, grow, and explore truth from a shared space of curiosity. We'll get into how to hold these honest dialogues in the coming chapters.

There are already some amazing grassroots movements that have made real strides in pushing truth and accountability. Take, for instance, the rise of community-based fact-checking organisations, which have popped up in response to the overwhelming amount of misinformation circulating on social media. These groups are made up of regular people who vet and fact-check news stories, making sure their neighbours, friends, and families aren't falling for fake headlines.

Other examples? Think about the success of local environmental activist groups that have fought to bring transparency to corporate pollution practices. These aren't groups with millions of followers on Instagram - they're real-world, boots-on-the-ground efforts that are shaking up industries and forcing corporations to be accountable.

What they all have in common is this; they recognise the power of community, collaboration, and collective effort in holding the line against deception. It's not just about one person spreading the word, it's about creating a whole network of informed, motivated individuals who can take action together. This is how truth becomes a movement.

If you're serious about fighting misinformation, you don't have to start big. It can be as simple as getting involved with existing truth-based communities or starting your own. Here's how you can get started:

1. Find or create local meet-ups. Whether it's a discussion group at your local library, a media literacy workshop at your community centre, or a monthly film screening that tackles misinformation, look for ways to create physical spaces where people can learn, discuss, and challenge each other's thinking. No, it doesn't need to be confrontational, but it does need to encourage people to think critically.

2. Start small with a book club or study group. Choose books that dive deep into media manipulation, psychological persuasion, politics, science or real world activism. Encourage people to read and discuss them together. This creates not only knowledge but also the sense of shared responsibility for spreading the truth.

3. Engage in non-confrontational activism. Start a petition about a local issue that's being misrepresented, or host a "truth talk" at your local coffee shop. The goal isn't to "win" the argument but to open the door to dialogue, helping people realise that they're not alone in

questioning the narratives they're fed.

4. Get active in local politics. If you're feeling bold, get involved in local politics or community advocacy. This is where real-world change happens. You don't have to run for office to make a difference. Volunteer for campaigns that advocate for truth, transparency, and accountability in both the media and politics.

5. Promote media literacy in your community. Use your social media platform to promote information about critical thinking, fact-checking, and identifying biassed sources. But don't just do it online - take the conversation offline, too. Offer to teach media literacy workshops in schools, libraries, or community centres. Teach people how to see through the noise and understand where information is coming from.

In the end, truth is a collective effort. It's not something we can fight for alone; we need each other. And when we come together - whether it's online or in the real world - we can shift the balance from misinformation to understanding, from confusion to clarity, and from chaos to connection.

Part 4: Taking Action

"The best way to predict the future is to create it." - Peter Drucker

We've covered the tricks, the lies, and the manipulation. We've exposed the system that allows it to thrive and taken a deep dive into how to spot the lies when they come at us. But knowing the truth is only half the battle. If we want to create real change, we have to act. It's time to take all that knowledge and apply it - to ourselves, to our communities, and to the systems that perpetuate these lies.

This part of the book isn't just about what you can do - it's about what you must do. It's about reclaiming your voice, questioning the status quo, and learning how to engage with others in a way that builds bridges instead of walls. The power to influence the narrative is in your hands, and it starts with taking action in your everyday life.

Whether you're debating with friends, influencing your local community, or using your voice online, the choices you make matter. This is your chance to be part of the solution, not just a passive bystander in a world awash with misinformation.

Let's look at how you can take everything you've learned and start making a difference - today.

Holding Media Accountable

Let's face it, the media isn't going to fix itself. The days of blindly trusting the nightly news or the headlines plastered across the papers are long gone. You've now got the power to spot bullshit when it's happening, but here's the next crucial step, holding the media accountable.

If we keep letting them slide, they'll keep feeding us more of the same lies, half-truths, and misdirection. So it's time to stop being passive consumers and start holding the media to a standard that respects truth, transparency, and ethical responsibility.

But how do you actually do that? It's easier than you think. Demanding accountability from media outlets starts with not accepting the status quo.

This doesn't mean yelling at the screen or throwing tantrums on social media. It means taking practical, real-world steps to let those in charge know that we're paying attention. The more we hold them accountable, the less power they'll have to push their agendas unchecked.

Demand Transparency

First things first, if a news outlet or media company can't be bothered to explain how they gather their information or what their editorial standards are, then why the hell are you bothering to trust them? The lack of transparency is a red flag. Media outlets have to be clear about how they find their content and if it's public information where they sourced it, who owns them, and what interests are driving their decisions. If they're not, they're operating in bad faith.

If you find yourself reading something that makes you go, "Hmm, something doesn't add up here," don't just swallow it. Question it. Look up who wrote the article, who funded it, and who benefits from spreading this message. When media outlets aren't transparent, they're basically telling you, "Trust us without question," and that's not how truth works. You deserve more than that.

Challenge Misinformation Effectively

It's not enough to just point at lies and say, "That's wrong." You need to challenge them in a way that forces a change. That means fact-checking. It means calling out contradictions, bad logic, and manipulative framing. And it means doing so in a way that's clear, respectful, and hard to ignore. A snarky Twitter comment isn't going to change anything. If you really want to make an impact, be articulate, be informed, and, most importantly, be relentless.

Sometimes, this can be as simple as writing a letter or submitting a complaint about false or misleading reporting. But don't just stop there. Take action, send an email, post on social media, use official complaint channels. Hold them accountable where it matters.

Most countries will have an industry standards board or organisation where you can lodge complaints to go above the media outlets themselves to where they're held accountable. You'll also often have similar organisations for advertising standards where you can report misleading commercials.

Don't let misleading headlines slide. Don't let outright lies pass without correction. Every time we don't call them out, we're tacitly giving permission for the next lie to be bigger and bolder. The more we do this, the less power they'll have to spread their harmful narratives unchecked.

Supporting Ethical Journalism and Advocating for Better Regulations

Look, mainstream media outlets are driven by profit, and their ratings drive the content they produce. Sensationalism sells, and so they will continue to profit off fear, outrage, and divisiveness. But ethical journalism isn't dead - it's just underfunded. So, support the outlets that make truth a priority. Support investigative journalism, independent reporting, and media that has a clear commitment to accuracy and transparency.

And don't just sit back and complain. Push for better regulations around misinformation and journalistic standards. Hold both media companies and tech giants accountable for the content they produce and spread. The next time you see a story that distorts facts, or a platform hosting blatant disinformation, use your voice to demand action.

The media landscape is being shaped by policies we can influence. But we have to show up, and we have to demand change. This isn't a time for complacency.

Hit 'em Where It Hurts

In a capitalist society, how do we best effect change? With the all mighty dollar. In this digital age it's us who are both the customer and the product. For the media outlets trying to hook us, and for the marketers and companies trying to sell to us, we're the customer. When their bottom line is affected they move. So if you spot media manipulation and deceptive practices, boycott them.

For the social media platforms, we are the product. So demand change, demand they move their platforms towards a better environment where truth and reasoned debate can thrive. If not, leave. Timothy Leary famously coined the phrase "Tune In, Turn On, Drop Out," in the sixties as a mantra for the hippie generation to sit up and take note. Well this generation's mantra should be "Logout, Delete, Reconnect." If you want to hit social media platforms where it hurts, then logout of their platform, delete their apps and reconnect with platforms pushing for positive change and real world community connections.

A mass exodus from the current systems will force change.

The Art of Honest Dialogue

Right here is one of my biggest pet peeves and the thing that drives me the most insane about the modern media and political environment. Put simply, the culture of debate today is broken. Everyone's so busy trying to "win" the argument that they forget to actually listen and understand the other side. Whether it's political spin, social media debates, or even family arguments at dinner, we've lost sight of the purpose of conversation, which is mutual understanding. It's about truth, not ego.

If we truly want to change minds and bring people back from the ideological extremes, we need to shift how we engage with one another. I believe the answer lies in one of the oldest forms of dialogue - Socratic questioning. Socrates, the father of critical thinking, taught that dialogue was not about defeating your opponent or proving you're right, but about reaching a deeper truth through careful, thoughtful questioning.

This approach is more than just a nice way to talk to people. It's a philosophy and a method that's more powerful than you may imagine. Here's why.

At the heart of modern debates, especially on social media, is the desire to win. Winning means scoring points, making the other side look dumb, and walking away with a supposed moral victory. But this is the Socratic paradox, where in trying to win, we end up losing. We lose the opportunity for growth, we lose the chance for understanding, and we lose the very thing that dialogue is meant to accomplish - truth.

Socrates himself was famously quoted for saying, "The only true wisdom is in knowing you know nothing." This is where the Socratic method starts. It's not about assuming you have the truth; it's about questioning your assumptions, probing the beliefs of others, and finding out where those beliefs might be flawed or incomplete. It's about openness, not certainty.

In contrast to the modern debate culture, Socratic questioning isn't designed to shut people down. It's about bringing them into a conversation that is as much about self-reflection as it is about exchange. The goal is not to prove the other person wrong, but to explore and expand the understanding of both parties.

For those of you who don't know Socrates, let's take a quick look back at history and I'm sure you'll start to see the parallels between the type of arguments and debates being had today and the revolutionary practice that Socrates himself applied back in the classical period of Greece.

Socrates lived between 469–399 BCE and was a Greek philosopher widely regarded as one of the founders of Western philosophy. He lived in Athens during what's known as its 'golden age' and was a key figure in shaping intellectual traditions that continue to this day.

Although he himself didn't write any of his teachings, so much of what we know comes from the writings of his students, particularly Plato and Xenophon, and later commentators like Aristotle. I'm sure at least some of these names are ringing a bell right?

In any case, Socrates' approach to philosophy was revolutionary for its emphasis on ethics, virtue, and the examination of one's own life. His famous dictum, "The unexamined life is not worth living," underscores his belief in constant self-inquiry and intellectual humility.

He spent much of his life engaging in public discourse in Athens, questioning citizens, politicians, and renowned thinkers alike. His method of inquiry, now known as the Socratic Method, involved asking probing questions to expose contradictions in others' beliefs, encouraging them to arrive at greater clarity and truth.

As with a lot of revolutionaries throughout history, sadly Socrates was eventually put on trial for impiety and corrupting the youth of Athens. When he was found guilty, he chose death over exile, drinking hemlock in a dramatic assertion of his philosophical principles. Quite literally a man who would die for his principles.

His main rivals, as you might call them, in these dialogues were known as The Sophists. These men were looked up to by the public as teachers and intellectuals in ancient Greece who specialised in rhetoric and taught people the skills of arguments and public speaking. While they were highly influential, they were often criticised for prioritising persuasion and sly tactics over truth.

These guys acted in a manner much like we see from many if not most of today's debaters and so-called intellectuals, where their goal was to use rhetoric to win points on their opponent and essentially make themselves look like grand masters of thought, while publicly shaming their opponents.

They were out to gain the admiration of the public and to humiliate those that chose to oppose them. These tactics would be implemented whether they truly believed in the argument or not, as many Sophists were relativists, believing that truth could be subjective or dependent on circumstances, so they'd change up their argument on a whim if it benefited their ego and resulted in them being seen as the winner.

Socrates on the other hand distinguished himself from the Sophists by emphasising the pursuit of objective truth rather than rhetorical skill. While Sophists were known to teach how to win arguments regardless of the ethical or logical validity of their stance, Socrates sought to uncover universal principles of virtue and morality.

For example, while a Sophist might argue that justice is whatever benefits the stronger party, Socrates would engage in a line of questioning to deconstruct this belief and explore what justice truly is.

Socrates employed a method of questioning designed to expose ignorance and force those that argued opposite to him to think critically, which Sophists didn't really do. They'd normally rely on their rhetoric, like surface level judgements, simple convincing sounding slogans and trickery with their words or phrasing.

In debates with Sophists, he often highlighted inconsistencies in their arguments by asking simple, logical questions. These questions weren't designed to make the Sophists look silly, or win points on them, but in a genuine search for the truth. Which in turn would generally infuriate the rhetoric laced Sophists and they'd trip up on their own lies.

Socrates rejected the Sophists' claim that truth is relative and varies from person to person, definitely not someone who would believe in "alternative facts." He argued for the existence of absolute truths, such as justice, virtue, and the good life, which could be discovered through reasoned inquiry.

And while Sophists often taught for monetary gain, aimed for political appointments or to live lavish lifestyles, Socrates considered philosophy a way of life and refused payment for his teachings. This commitment to his ideals gave him moral authority in debates, contrasted with the perceived cynicism of the Sophists.

The legacy of Socrates' confrontations with the Sophists represent a foundational struggle between philosophy as the pursuit of truth and rhetoric as the art of persuasion. His critiques of Sophistic relativism and shallow argumentation laid the groundwork for ethical philosophy and logical reasoning, principles that still to this very day remain central to critical thinking.

Contrast this Socratic Method and dialogue with Sophists to the type of confrontations we see today in all levels of debate especially on social media and worst still in politics. No one today is truly engaged in dialogue in the way that Socrates would be proud of. And while the meaning of 'sophisticated' may not have true etymological roots back to the term 'Sophists', I can't help but look at a lot of modern day pundits and politicians and remark at how 'sophisticated' they are.

The world is full of rhetoric, everyone out to simply be seen scoring points on others. Professional debaters will often use the exact style of the ancient Sophists, filled with purposeful mischaracterisations, misrepresentations, and tricky language simply to be seen as the victor. It's like everyone picks a side and then carefully learns the talking points that best make a fool of their opponent.

Politicians don't stand opposite each other in a debate steeped in the search for compromise and truth, as I'm sure you'd know if you've ever watched your country's version of C-SPAN. Because you'd be forgiven if you had thought you'd tuned into a school yard dispute between five year old, emotionally immature children.

When have you ever seen a politician agree with an opposition party and work towards the goal of an agreeable compromise? In the US, the supposed model of democracy and the shining light of the free world, Democrats and Republicans staunchly stand opposed to each other now more than ever. The increased use of the filibuster is a prime example of this, they'd rather talk endlessly about nothing in order to delay a vote, or block a bill passing, rather than engaging in dialogue to work towards a better future.

The evolution of how television and social media operate have also given rise to more exaggerated versions of this winner vs loser approach. When pundits are brought onto news shows these segments are often run tightly, with little time given to flesh out an argument, so it simply devolves into a battle of who can talk over the other, and now more than ever who can get that "viral moment."

This same rhetoric then filters down to the general public, like think about it. When have you ever seen someone have their minds changed in a comment thread on social media? I know myself I can count maybe once or twice in all my life have I seen someone who genuinely seems to have changed their view during a comment section argument.

The reason no-one changes their mind, is because no-one likes being made to look like a fool. If you leave no room for the fundamental pursuit of truth in your life, and can only stand by shallow arguments, then you'd sooner resort to name calling or violence then be seen as the loser in a debate.

This is where we as consumers, as the viewers, the commenters, need to hold ourselves accountable. Because we are the ones that cause these clips to go viral, we are the ones who vote for the politicians and we are the ones who parrot the talking points or move the goalposts until we can walk away feeling like we or our side won. So next time you find yourself in a situation where you recognise a debate of ideas is occurring, approach it with the philosophy of Socrates and seek truth through understanding.

This very thing, the us vs them rhetoric, will be the demise of our civilisation if we don't curb our habits to suit a more progressive method in line with that of the way Socrates would approve.

Socratic dialogue is more than just a technique - it's a mindset. Instead of seeing the other person as an enemy to defeat, you approach them as a fellow truth-seeker. Socrates believed that wisdom comes from shared inquiry and that through careful questioning, both people could learn more about themselves and the world.

One of the biggest strengths of the Socratic method is that it encourages active listening. In modern debate culture, we often "listen" to respond, not to understand. The Socratic method, on the other hand, demands active listening - you can't ask meaningful questions if you haven't fully heard and understood the other person's position.

When people feel like they're being listened to, they're more likely to engage honestly and possibly even reconsider their stance. A Socratic dialogue is about examining beliefs and allowing both sides to do so with respect and humility.

One of the most powerful examples of Socratic dialogue in action came during the American Civil Rights Movement, particularly in the Deep South. When Martin Luther King Jr. and other activists engaged with white segregationists, they weren't trying to "win" in the typical sense. Instead, they were trying to open minds through conversation and questioning.

In many cases, these dialogues took place in jails, bus rides, and even public meetings where King's followers would ask questions that forced the opposition to examine their own beliefs. When Dr. King wrote his "Letter from Birmingham Jail," he wasn't just responding to his critics - he was engaging with them on a deeper level. He used questions to challenge the idea of "gradualism" and to force his critics to question their own biases, urging them to reflect on justice and morality.

What made it work so well was that the dialogue wasn't an attack, but an exploration of truth. King and his fellow activists understood that changing hearts and minds requires empathy, respect, and the willingness to question assumptions. The Socratic approach allowed them to challenge deep-seated racist beliefs by showing the moral inconsistency of segregationist practices.

At the end of the day whether it's addressing systemic injustice, ending violent conflict, combating misinformation, or bridging political divides, honest dialogue can be the key to progress. The humility in understanding that true knowledge exists in knowing that you know nothing, and the willingness to engage in dialogue with an open mind, is what makes the Socratic method so powerful.

Toolkit for Practicing Honest, Constructive Conversations

1. Start by listening - actively and openly. Don't prepare your response while the other person is speaking; actually hear them out.

2. Ask questions - don't attack. Challenge their thinking by asking questions that encourage them to reflect on their beliefs and assumptions.

3. Be patient and respectful. Remember, this is a conversation, not a competition. Give the other person space to explain their point of view without interrupting.

4. Follow up with clarity. When you ask a question, ensure it's focused on understanding the truth, not on trapping them. Ask for specifics, and encourage them to explain further.

5. Know when to agree. Sometimes, agreeing is the most powerful way to keep the conversation moving forward. Find the areas where you both agree, and build from there.

6. Stay open. Be willing to change your mind if the evidence or the conversation leads you there. This isn't about winning or losing; it's about learning.

7. Stay calm. When conversations get heated, keep your emotions in check. This isn't about proving your worth or winning the argument; it's about learning and understanding.

The Socratic method isn't a silver bullet. It doesn't guarantee that you'll change people's minds overnight, or even at all. But it does create the space for honest, respectful dialogue that encourages real understanding. In a world where divisiveness and outrage reign, it's time we bring back meaningful conversations that lead to growth - for ourselves and for society as a whole.

The Educated Rebel

"In times of universal deceit, telling the truth is a revolutionary act." - George Orwell

Okay, we've covered a lot in this book and it's easy to feel small in the face of the overwhelming machinery of lies, manipulation, and media spin. But here's the truth, you are more powerful than you think.

The reality is that truth is not something we're going to magically stumble upon. It's something we have to actively fight for, day in and day out. You don't need to be a journalist or an expert to make a difference. You just need to be a conscious consumer of information and a passionate advocate for truth.

Inspiring a Revolution of Truth

We're living in a world where it's easier than ever to get swept up in the lies. Fake news, viral hoaxes, biased media - these things aren't just affecting the fringe of society anymore. They're everywhere. They're affecting you, your friends, your family, and the very fabric of society. But you're not powerless in this, you have a choice. You can either continue to let the noise wash over you, or you can become an educated rebel.

An educated rebel isn't someone who just reads the headlines and scrolls past everything else. They're the ones who ask questions. They're the ones who refuse to be part of the herd.

They challenge the status quo, not by shouting louder, but by speaking with integrity, by promoting critical thinking, and by demanding better from the media, politicians, and companies who shape our lives.

In a world where lying has become the norm, truth-telling is the act of rebellion. And it starts with you.

Resisting Misinformation and Building Resilience

I'm not talking about becoming a crusader who argues with everyone at Thanksgiving dinner (you don't want to end up the crazy Aunt or Uncle at family events). What I'm talking about is building up the resilience to resist misinformation. You see, it's not about fighting every battle - it's about knowing when to push back and how to keep your own mind sharp and protected from the ever-present stream of manipulative content.

You'll need to develop a few key traits:

1. Critical thinking. Stop accepting things at face value. Ask questions. Challenge your own assumptions.

2. Emotional resilience. Understand that being constantly exposed to misleading content can trigger fear, anger, or frustration. Don't let it dictate your response.

3. Active listening. Sometimes, the best way to cut through misinformation is not to correct someone right away, but to listen, understand where they're coming from, and offer thoughtful insights.

The good news is that this resilience is not only for you. It can spread. When you take the time to break down and question what you hear and share, you start a ripple effect. You'll begin to inspire others to think critically, to fight against misinformation, and to be better consumers of media. The truth can spread faster than a viral hoax - only if we give it the chance.

There's a great saying that a client of mine taught me, "The rising tide, lifts all of the boats," so be a part of that tide by raising your own standards, and others will follow.

A Personal Action Plan for Promoting Truth

Here's where we get into the nitty-gritty of what you're going to do with all this newfound knowledge. If you want to be an educated rebel, you've got to start somewhere. So, let's break it down.

1. Start with yourself.
   Before you can challenge the system, you've got to arm yourself with the tools to see it clearly. Curate your media and stop mindlessly scrolling. Choose reputable sources and actively diversify your news. Take the time to educate yourself on how media works, how misinformation spreads, and what propaganda really looks like. Don't be satisfied with a surface-level understanding of anything.

2. Educate others.
   It doesn't take a Ph.D. to start conversations about misinformation. Start with your close circle, friends, family, colleagues. Ask questions. Share insights. Encourage them to think critically. Then use social media responsibly. Don't just share posts that resonate emotionally. Share information that educates, challenges, and opens minds. Create opportunities for dialogue, you'd be surprised how many people are open to conversations when the space provided is one based in honesty and respect. Look for moments to create those spaces - whether it's in person or online.

3. Support ethical media.
You don't have to go it alone. Subscribe to independent outlets and support those who are committed to quality journalism and truth. Then hold others accountable, don't just let biased news slip by. Demand better from the sources you rely on.

4. Get involved offline.
I get it - the internet is where it all happens, but the real work is done in communities. Join local groups focused on media literacy or fact-checking. Attend town hall meetings, engage in local politics, and create space for thoughtful debate and critical thinking in your community. Build coalitions with others who are committed to fighting misinformation. The more voices we have, the more powerful we become.

The Big Picture: We Can Win This

This is about more than just fighting back against fake news or misleading advertising practises. This is about creating a culture of truth - one where manipulation, lies, and doublespeak no longer have a place. We've been sold a lie for too long that we're powerless, that we can't make a difference. But that's simply not true. Your voice matters.

Every time you ask the right questions, every time you challenge the narrative, every time you share the truth with someone who didn't know it before, you win. And with every win, the tide turns a little further toward the truth. And one day, we'll look back and say, "We were the generation that fought for the truth and came out on top."

So, go ahead. Be the rebel. Start today.

Part 5: The Role of AI – Promise and Peril

"The real question is not whether machines think but whether men do." - B.F. Skinner

As artificial intelligence continues to evolve at breakneck speed, it's no longer a question of if AI will reshape our world - it already is. From the algorithms shaping the content we consume to the bots spreading propaganda on social media, AI's influence is undeniable. The digital age has introduced a whole new set of tools to manipulate and control narratives, and AI is the cutting-edge weapon in that arsenal.

But here's the twist, the true danger of AI isn't necessarily that it will surpass human intelligence, it's that it's already being used to magnify our worst impulses. Whether it's fine-tuning our biases or creating convincing deepfakes, AI has the power to deceive on a scale previously unimaginable. We are now in a position where machines, programmed by humans, have the ability to control the flow of information, amplify lies, and perpetuate illusions of truth. The question is no longer about what AI can do, but what it will do - and who will benefit from its vast capabilities.

In this final part of the book, we'll explore the promise and peril of AI's impact on media, truth, and deception. From its revolutionary potential to its dark side, we'll dive deep into the role AI plays in shaping the narratives we hear, see, and believe - and how it could either free us or further entrap us in a web of manipulation.

The Perils of AI in Misinformation

If you thought the problem of fake news was bad now, just wait until AI becomes a full-blown misinformation machine. We're on the brink of a new era where technology can create lies so convincing that it'll be nearly impossible to tell what's real and what's not. And make no mistake - this is no sci-fi fantasy. It's happening right now. Welcome to the perils of AI.

Deepfakes: The Erosion of Trust in Visual Evidence

Deepfakes are not just a funny party trick anymore. They're a legitimate threat to our entire perception of reality. Think about it, we've always trusted images and videos as "proof," right? We see it on the news, in documentaries, and social media. But now, AI can manipulate that visual evidence, replacing faces, voices, and actions with total ease. These fakes don't just exist in the realm of celebrities and conspiracy theories - they're already being used in political campaigns, and in the future, they could be a part of everything from corporate warfare to personal vendettas.

Some movie studios have already started to incorporate this technology into blockbuster films and TV shows. As an example in recent Disney Star Wars shows they've used it to replace the face of a stand in actor and bring a young Luke Skywalker back to screen in such a realistic way that you could almost swear they pulled him directly out of a time machine from the seventies. They used it in integration with other technology and there were still some uncanny valley vibes to it, but if Disney are starting to use it, you have to worry about what else it will be used in as the technology advances.

The problem is, the more these deepfakes become widespread, the less we're going to trust anything we see. Visual evidence was once the gold standard for truth. We've discussed earlier in the book how that is affected simply by the craft of us humans, but now with AI? A video of someone saying or doing something may not be evidence at all - it might just be a well-crafted piece of AI manipulation. And as these deepfakes get more realistic, the danger is that we'll end up doubting all video evidence, even when it's authentic.

GPT Models: Crafting Convincing, Yet False, Narratives

Next up are GPT models, the AI-powered writing systems that have already revolutionised content creation. And while they're great for drafting blog posts or generating product descriptions, they're a double-edged sword. These models can write persuasive, coherent narratives - even if those narratives are complete and utter bullshit.

Think about it, an AI can now write an article that looks completely legitimate, from structure to style. It can pull from massive data sets to create what seems like well-researched, thoughtful analysis. But here's the catch, it doesn't have a clue about what's true or false. It's just generating patterns based on previous data. So when these models are fed misinformation or biased data, they simply repeat it. They can write false narratives with the same fluency as an expert, and that makes them incredibly dangerous.

The GPT models are already being put to use at scale across the internet and writers across the film industry have even gone on strike to demand movie studios and television networks have strict limitations around the use of such tech in order to safeguard their own jobs.

But the concern isn't just based around creative industries, what happens when a GPT model is tasked with writing a political article that manipulates public sentiment, spreads propaganda, or outright lies? The answer is unfortunately something you may find terrifying, a new era of mass misinformation, automated at scale.

Next-Gen Images and Video

If you thought deepfakes were the end of our visual troubles, you're sadly mistaken. For in just the past few years the rise of "next-gen" AI video and image generation has excelled at breakneck speeds.

Companies like MidJourney, Flux, Runway AI and the soon to be released Sora have seen phenomenal advances in their generational ability. It seems like only yesterday when these tools first hit the market and they seemed like novel ideas, but definitely lacked the realism needed to convince anyone that the images and videos they produced were from the real world. They would struggle with correct texture and lighting, teeth and hands would often be a jumbled mess, and god forbid if you asked them to generate a human eating food - truly some nightmarish results.

But now as of the writing of this book, you can create images so lifelike and define details right down to the exact style of camera that took the image that it's close to impossible for the average person, even experts, to pick what is a real photo anymore.

Only a year ago the video capabilities were such poor quality that anyone could tell it was AI. There was a grainy quality to a lot of it, the generations were only very short and there was often a morphing that would occur - again to some nightmarish results.

Today, not only can you generate lifelike photos and then use those to generate incredibly lifelike videos, you can use tools to direct the movement in the scene and use AI generated voices to insert dialogue. It's truly at such production level standards that only days ago Coca-Cola released their first ever fully AI generated video commercial for their Christmas holiday campaign. Which is traditionally a campaign backed with gigantic budgets the size of a small country's entire GDP.

And the release of OpenAI's new video model Sora is being much anticipated, with the company showcasing a range of videos that have even the tech experts debating if they're somehow cheating because the results are almost too lifelike. So you really do need to question everything you see and hear.

Weaponising AI: Propaganda and Targeted Disinformation

The real danger lies in weaponising AI. We're talking about using these technologies to deliberately spread disinformation and manipulate entire populations. Think about how AI could be used to generate fake news stories, create fake social media accounts to amplify certain narratives, or target specific groups with tailored misinformation campaigns. This is no longer about a single bot on Twitter spewing nonsense; this is about AI-driven propaganda on a massive scale, designed to exploit every emotional trigger, every fear, and every bias.

Governments, organisations, and individuals with a lot of resources can now deploy AI to push their own agendas in ways that are indistinguishable from real, human-run operations. In a world where truth is already fragile, the introduction of AI-powered disinformation could destroy what's left of our trust in the media, in politicians, and in each other.

Take for example in elections, which are already a hotbed for misinformation, when you throw AI into the mix, things get downright scary. In 2016, AI-powered bots played a major role in the U.S. Presidential election. These bots weren't just spamming social media with random tweets; they were designed to target specific voters, spread fake stories, and amplify divisive narratives. In essence, they manipulated emotions and opinions in ways that traditional media never could.

What makes this particularly insidious is how AI can pinpoint the exact moment when a voter is most vulnerable to manipulation. The algorithms used by social media platforms can track what users are reading, what they're engaging with, and how they're feeling based on their browsing behaviour. From there, AI can deliver hyper-targeted content designed to provoke anger, fear, or division. For instance, one study showed that certain countries (who will remain nameless for my own protection) employed AI tools to create fake accounts that impersonated real Americans, organising rallies and protests - sometimes promoting opposite political agendas at the same time - to deepen polarisation. These bots didn't just spread lies - they exploited the emotional vulnerabilities of entire populations, leaving them susceptible to influence.

The danger here is that the use of AI in elections makes misinformation so sophisticated that it can blend in with real discourse. If a voter can't distinguish between truth and AI-fuelled fiction, they become the perfect target for manipulation.

AI Amplifying Hate Speech and Fake News

The other side of this coin is AI amplifying hate speech and fake news on a global scale. AI algorithms are engineered to prioritise content that gets engagement, which means they often boost the most emotionally charged, inflammatory, or controversial posts. Unfortunately, hate speech, misinformation, and extremist ideologies tend to fit these criteria perfectly.

Take YouTube's recommendation algorithm, for example. It has been shown that AI-driven recommendations sometimes push users down rabbit holes of extreme content. One study found that after watching a few seemingly innocuous videos, YouTube's algorithm was more likely to suggest videos from far-right extremists, conspiracy theorists, and even terrorist sympathisers. Similarly, Facebook's algorithm has been used to spread fake news stories and amplify hate speech.

AI's role here isn't just about creating false content; it's about amplifying it, enabling it to spread faster and wider than ever before. AI doesn't have the morality to say, "Hey, maybe spreading this kind of hate is a bad idea." It just follows the rules of engagement - keep the user interacting, keep the content viral, and keep the profits rolling.

Tips for Recognising AI-Generated Content and Questioning Its Reliability

Alright, let's get real for a second. How do you tell when AI is behind something? How can you spot when a piece of content - be it a video, an article, or even a social media post - is not just misleading, but engineered to deceive?

1. Check the Source. AI might generate convincing narratives, but the source matters. If you're reading something that feels too polished or too perfect, it could be AI-generated. Look for reputable sources, websites with clear editorial standards, and avoid content from nameless platforms or fake-looking sites.

2. Analyse the Tone. AI is still terrible at nuance. If a piece of content feels robotic or lacks human empathy - if it reads more like a manual or a script than something personal - it's probably AI-generated. Human writers have quirks. We add personality, humour, or emotion into what we create. AI, however, is emotionless and mechanical. It might sound factual but often feels emotionally shallow. Pay attention to that.

3. Reverse-Image Search. This is particularly useful when it comes to visuals. Deepfakes and AI-generated images often have inconsistencies in the lighting, shadows, or background that are hard to spot at first glance. Use reverse-image search tools like Google Image Search or TinEye to verify if an image has been altered or artificially created. If it's a fake, you'll likely find traces of it elsewhere on the internet.

4. Fact-Check the Facts. AI can write a decent article, but it can't always check the facts. If you come across something that feels off, fact-check it. Use reliable fact-checking websites like Snopes, PolitiFact, or even check the data in reputable databases. AI-generated articles sometimes mix up numbers, take quotes out of context, or create "facts" from thin air. It's often sloppy if you dig deep enough.

5. Follow the Money. AI doesn't care about truth; it cares about engagement and profit. Be skeptical of content that's trying to sell you something - especially if it's AI-generated. If the content seems like a plug for a product or service without any substance behind it, the chances are high that it's designed for one thing - profit.

By arming yourself with these tools, you can start to see through the AI-generated bullshit that's becoming more prevalent. The key is questioning everything - especially the content that seems too good (or too outrageous) to be true. Because when it comes to AI, the truth can be easily twisted, and it's up to you to recognise it before it's too late.

The Promise of AI in Truth-Seeking

AI has a dark side, no doubt. But, here's the thing that often gets overlooked, AI is not inherently bad. Like any tool, it's about how we use it. And when we use it to fight the very misinformation that AI has helped spread, we start to see its potential for good.

Just think about it - AI can be our ally in the fight for truth. It can help us fact-check faster, debunk false claims in real time, and give us the tools to identify bias in media coverage. And, let's face it, we need all the help we can get.

AI Tools for Fact-Checking and Debunking False Claims in Real Time

Imagine you're scrolling through your feed and you come across a headline that makes your blood boil - let's say it's about some "breaking news" that fits perfectly with your worldview. How can we know if it's complete bullshit or not? What if, instead of reading it and blindly sharing it, AI could instantly tell you whether the claim is true or not?

That's what's happening with real-time fact-checking tools. AI systems, powered by natural language processing and machine learning, are already being used to scan news articles, videos, and social media posts to check for false claims. These tools scan the web for contradictions, identify unreliable sources, and can even pull up the actual data or studies behind a claim. Instead of waiting for the traditional fact-checkers to get to it (which, let's face it, could take days), AI could act as a first line of defence.

You'd get an instant "fact-check" pop-up to show you whether something's real or fabricated.

One tool you might recognise is ClaimBuster, an AI-based platform designed to check the factual accuracy of political statements. It's not perfect yet, but it's a huge step in the right direction. Deep learning models can already cross-reference claims with reliable databases and alert readers to discrepancies, so the potential here is massive - imagine a world where we're armed with instant verification of any claim we come across, be pretty cool right?

Here's the thing, AI isn't just about spotting lies. It can also help us identify bias - in real time. Think about how machine learning can analyse massive datasets to pinpoint skewed language, selective reporting, or framing tactics that have been used in news coverage.

That's right, AI can call out media bias in a way that humans can't. Traditional fact-checking sites or watchdog organisations might take days or even weeks to assess a news report. But machine learning can scan hundreds of articles, looking for patterns of bias or manipulation. In a split second, you could know whether a story is being framed from a left-wing or right-wing bias, or if a source is cherry-picking data to support a specific narrative.

This kind of transparency in reporting could completely revolutionise the media landscape, making it harder for outlets to spin the truth in ways that align with their political or corporate interests. Instead of being stuck in a cycle of "he said, she said," AI can provide a clearer picture of what's actually happening.

Of course, none of this matters if AI is developed and used without ethics in mind. If we're not careful, we could end up trading one form of manipulation for another. And that's where ethical AI comes in.

The best way forward is for engineers and policymakers to prioritise truth in their AI designs. We need AI systems that actively seek transparency, accountability, and truthfulness. These systems should be transparent in how they operate, and they should be built with fairness and objectivity in mind. Developers need to prioritise ethical standards to avoid AI becoming just another tool for manipulation. A world where AI can analyse data ethically and expose biases in reporting could change the game when it comes to media accountability.

As an example AI is already being used in journalism to help analyse large datasets for investigative reporting. Journalists at places like The New York Times or Reuters are using AI tools to scan thousands of documents, analyse patterns, and even help uncover stories that would have been impossible to find manually. The use of AI in these contexts isn't just about making life easier - it's about getting closer to the truth faster, and with more accuracy.

How You Can Support and Use AI Tools Designed for Truth and Accountability

Okay, let's not pretend like this all sounds great without a little action behind it. Here's how you - yes, you - can get in on the good side of AI.

1. Use Fact-Checking Tools. There are plenty of fact-checking tools powered by AI that you can start using today. ClaimBuster, as mentioned earlier, is one such tool. Others include PolitiFact and FactCheck.org, both of which are starting to incorporate AI into their processes. Make these tools a part of your daily routine. Before you

share a post, run it through one of these sites. Start pushing back on misinformation when you spot it.

2. Support Ethical AI Developers. Not all AI is created equal. When you have the chance, support organisations and companies that are prioritising ethical AI development. These are the ones creating tools that fight misinformation instead of amplifying it. They might not be as flashy or as profitable as the big tech giants, but they're doing the right thing. Look for AI startups or nonprofits focused on transparency, objectivity, and accountability.

3. Push for Regulation. We can't just sit back and hope for the best. We need to push policymakers to regulate AI in ways that prioritise truth. If you're really passionate about combating misinformation, start pushing for policies that require AI companies to disclose how their algorithms work and how they handle misinformation. Supporting transparency regulations is the first step in making AI a force for good.

4. Get Involved with AI for Social Good. AI isn't just for big corporations. There are initiatives like AI for Good that focus on using AI to solve global challenges, including misinformation. Get involved. Support those efforts. Use your voice to advocate for AI that helps people, not harms them.

The key here is simple. AI can be a tool for truth, transparency, and accountability - but only if we push for it. You have the power to influence this shift, so start using AI ethically and supporting those who are building it with integrity. It's time to turn the tide on misinformation, and AI might just be the ally we've been waiting for.

The Dual-Edged Sword of AI in Media

As we've explored, AI is not a force of nature - it's a tool, and like any tool, its power depends on how we use it. On one hand, AI has the potential to be an incredible ally in the fight for truth. It can expose biases, debunk misinformation in real time, and help journalists uncover hidden patterns that were once buried in mountains of data. If we use it wisely, AI can illuminate the truth in ways we never thought possible, bringing much-needed transparency and fairness to the media landscape.

But on the other hand, the same technology that can help us seek the truth can also be weaponised to deceive, manipulate, and mislead. Deepfakes, synthetic news, and AI-driven propaganda are already wreaking havoc on public trust, spreading misinformation faster than we can even begin to process it. In an age where information travels at the speed of light, we're at risk of drowning in a sea of digital lies unless we stay vigilant.

Here's the thing, AI is a reflection of us - it learns from the data we feed it. If we're not careful, it can perpetuate the same biases, distortions, and deceit that have plagued traditional media for years. The key difference now is that AI can do it on a much larger scale, at speeds and volumes that we can't even fathom.

So, what's the answer? It's up to us. It's up to you, to me, to everyone who cares about the truth. We can't sit back and hope that AI just magically works for the good of humanity. We need to take proactive steps to make sure it's used ethically, transparently, and in ways that prioritise truth over profit or political agendas. The future of AI, especially in the media, isn't just in the hands of engineers and corporations - it's in ours too.

In an AI-driven era, media literacy is no longer optional. We need to question everything. We need to understand how algorithms shape what we see and hear, and we need to hold those who wield AI accountable for the narratives they craft. The responsibility is ours to not only use these tools wisely but also to ensure that they serve the greater good.

It's going to take vigilance. It's going to take effort. But it's not impossible. With the right tools, knowledge, and awareness, we can ensure that AI becomes a force for good, not a tool for manipulation. It's about being proactive, ethical, and above all, committed to the truth. The future of media, both online and offline, is in our hands.

Conclusion: Rebuilding Trust, One Truth at a Time

You've made it. You've journeyed through the mess of media manipulation, deception, and the wild world of misinformation. You hopefully now understand more about how the system works, how to spot the lies, and how to demand better. You've armed yourself with the tools of media literacy. But now comes the real question - What are you going to do with all this knowledge?

The answer is simple. Use it.

It's time to stop sitting back and letting the world fall apart. This isn't a spectator sport - this is your life, your future, and your ability to make sense of the madness around you. The skills you've learned throughout this book are useless if you don't use them to cut through the noise, expose the deception, and rebuild a culture of truth. It's time to be the truth-teller, the truth-seeker, and the truth-builder.

You don't have to be a media mogul, a journalist, or an expert in AI to make an impact. You don't need to be perfect. You don't need to win every argument. But you do need to hold yourself accountable - and the media, the platforms, the people who spread lies - accountable too. If you want to change things, start by questioning everything. Every headline. Every statistic. Every "fact." And don't just stop there. If you see something that doesn't smell right, call it out. Demand better. Demand transparency. If the truth matters, say so.

We can't rely on big corporations, governments, or tech giants to fix the media landscape. That responsibility falls on us - on every single one of us who cares enough to make a difference. You have the power to change the world, but it starts with changing how you interact with the world. Start by questioning, learning, and acting. Be the person who doesn't just consume information but actively engages with it.

But let's be clear, this won't be easy. Deception is everywhere. Media giants will try to drown you in a sea of lies, distractions, and misinformation. It'll be frustrating. It'll feel like you're up against a wall sometimes. But the truth is, that wall is just made of lies and it's crumbling down. It's up to us to push through it.

As you leave this book, know that you're not just a passive consumer anymore. You're part of the solution. Every time you call out a lie, every time you refuse to fall for a narrative, every time you seek the truth even when it's inconvenient or uncomfortable, you are rebuilding trust in something that's been broken. One truth at a time.

The world may be messy. The media may be full of noise. But you now have the skills to cut through it. You have the power to see the truth, spot the lies, and demand better. So get out there and use it. Don't sit on the sidelines.

The fight for truth doesn't end with this book. It begins here. It begins with you.

It's time to take action.